The Holy Spirit

The Holy Spirit

C. F. D. Moule

Wipf & Stock
PUBLISHERS
Eugene, Oregon

Wipf and Stock Publishers
199 W 8th Ave, Suite 3
Eugene, OR 97401

The Holy Spirit
By Moule, C. F. D.
Copyright©1978 Cassell
ISBN: 1-57910-035-X
Publication date 5/7/1997

I. Setting the Stage

IT would not be difficult to write in general terms about some of the ways in which God has worked and is still at work among men and women. But the aim of this book is to look mainly at distinctively Christian positions and, within this area, to adhere as strictly as possible to those aspects of God's work, and those alone, which may most properly be described in terms of the Spirit of God. The subject is specifically the Spirit of God in Christian doctrine and experience; and although so living and flexible a theme would be killed dead by any sort of rigidity in treatment the attempt is made throughout to keep to the subject and not to wander indiscriminately—even within the bounds of Christian thought—over the theme of God's mighty deeds in general.

Not that the word 'spirit' is not itself an invitation to ramble. It is so widely and loosely used in religious talk today that a commission to write a book on the subject is about as informative as saying 'Write an essay on air'. (As it happens, of course, 'air', or, at any rate, 'wind', is one of the meanings of 'spirit'. But that is by the way.) Most people who use religious language at all use 'spirit' as the opposite of 'matter': for them, the word denotes, in the vaguest and most general way, whatever transcends the material or belongs to 'the other world'.[1] 'A spirit' might mean a spectre or a ghost (and 'ghost' is etymologically akin to 'Geist', the German for 'spirit'). The Bible, however, for the most part uses the words rendered by 'spirit' in a more restricted and more specialized way. This is largely true both of what Christians call the Old Testament (the Jewish canonical scriptures in Hebrew and Aramaic) and of the New Testament (the distinctively Christian scriptures written in Greek). Some of the Jewish writings just outside and

1

subsequent to the Old Testament use the word in wider and less typically biblical ways. But in all the canonical writings, despite their wide variety, the usage is, in the main, strikingly specialized and restricted; and in the New Testament in particular, 'the Holy Spirit' takes on a special meaning.

In examining the biblical roots of Christian understandings of the Spirit, we encounter another surprising limitation. In the language of post-biblical Christian devotion, the Holy Spirit has often been associated with fiery zeal and zest. In 'Come, Holy Ghost, our souls inspire'—a free rendering by the seventeenth century bishop, John Cosin, of the ancient hymn *Veni, Creator Spiritus*—we meet 'celestial fire' and 'fire of love' (though, to be sure, in the original there is nothing corresponding to 'fire' in the first occurrence, and even in the second, 'fire' is a separate aspect, side by side with 'love', and not linked to love as in Cosin's version). Again, from the contemporary scene, Ian M. Fraser writes a book called *The Fire Runs* (London: SCM 1975), and says in it, 'the fire of the Holy Spirit is running through the world' (p. 68). Fire seems to us a natural symbol for zeal and energy and contagious enthusiasm. 'He has no fire in his belly', we say of a lifeless speaker; or, 'the news spread like wild fire'. But here, again, biblical usage is more restricted. Sometimes 'fire' and 'spirit' do come together; but fire turns out to be a metaphor for destruction rather than for zeal. In James 3.5 an uncontrolled tongue can start a disastrous blaze, like a spark in a timber yard. Sometimes it is destruction for a constructive purpose, like the refiner's fire which separates the dross from the precious metal. At Isaiah's call, his lips are touched and purged with a burning coal from the altar (Isa. 6.5–7). Or it is like a fire which consumes what is cheap and perishable to clear a space for what is durable. But in any case it is judgement—a powerful metaphor for divine judgement. If it is a correct gospel tradition which represents John the Baptist as saying that his great Successor would baptize with fire as well as with Holy Spirit (Matt. 3.11, Luke 3.16—cf. Isa. 4.4; not Mark 1.8, John 1.33, Acts 1.5), it is possible that this meant that the Holy Spirit would act like a refiner's fire,[2] or, alternatively, that the experience would be like the process of winnowing, in which the wind (the same word as spirit, in Greek and Hebrew) blows away the chaff, and fire consumes it.[3] In a saying peculiar to Luke (12.49 ff.), to the effect that Jesus had come to cast fire on the earth (or to set fire to it?), the fire seems to mean the 'flaming' antagonism and dissension caused within families when one member responds to the demands of the sovereignty of God and the others do not. But rarely, if ever, is 'fire' used in the Bible to denote enthusiasm. The nearest it comes to this is when, in St Luke's wonderful story of the walk to Emmaus, the two disciples speak of how their heart was kindled (literally, 'burning', 'aflame') as they listened to the unrecognized stranger (Luke 24.32). Even here, it could conceivably be, like Jeremiah's fire in his bones (Jer. 20.9), something that had to be let out and uttered; or it might even be the fire of judgement in their hearts, as they began to realize how they had themselves misjudged the situation; but this seems less likely. It seems to be a rare example of fire as a metaphor for excitement or zeal. The comparable metaphor of 'boiling' does indeed seem to be used to suggest verve and enthusiasm, in Acts 18.25 (of Apollos) and in Rom. 12.11 (both these, in association with the word 'spirit'—or 'Spirit'?); and, without reference to the Spirit, the Christians of Laodicea are accused, in Rev. 3.14 ff., of being neither cold nor hot but lukewarm. The 'tongues as though of fire' at Pentecost (Acts 2.3) might also be meant to suggest enthusiasm; but perhaps more probably this signifies a divine visitation, like the burning bush of Exod. 3.2, perhaps like the fiery pillar of the wilderness wanderings (Num. 9.15 ff., etc), and like the mysterious fire in such scenes as the encounters with a divine visitant in Judges 6.21, and 13.20, or like Elijah's fire from heaven, 1 Kings 18.38, 2 Kings 1.9 ff.[4] Hardly relevant here is the metaphor of being on fire with uncontrollable lust (1 Cor. 7.9), or of rekindling a fire that has sunk low (Phil. 4.10, 2 Tim. 1.6); but the destructive fires of Jerusalem's perpetual incinerator, the Valley called Gehinnom, which became a symbol for the destruction of human personality (Gehenna), represent in extreme form the negative associations of fire (Isa. 66.24, Mark 9.48, etc).

Thus, current language about the Spirit's fervour may turn out to be less essential than might be imagined. But this is in no way to question the reality of the stupendous power or divine magnificence of the Spirit's presence, or the zest and zeal that can result. Nor need it suggest that fire is not now an appropriate metaphor for zeal. Different metaphors obtain at different periods. Jesus himself evidently introduced metaphors and images and parables in his own teaching which were new and supremely effective vehicles for messages which, in his own Scriptures, were conveyed in other ways. What matters is to understand how words are used in different documents, and to explore, as reverently and precisely as possible, what is distinctive in Christian understandings of the Spirit of God. To experience the power of the Spirit is obviously far more important than to talk about it. Yet it does matter what one believes, and the attempt to understand the experiences and their origins, as far as such deep mysteries permit, is of practical importance. The understanding of God's actions in our own day and the ability to respond to them with intelligent and eager obedience depends not a little on understanding whence and how we have been brought to where we are.

When Christians speak of 'the Holy Spirit' (or, in Elizabethan English, 'the Holy Ghost'—*not* meaning a spectre), they often mean an eternal aspect of God: they mean the third 'person' of the Holy Trinity, alongside God the Father and God the Son. ('Person' is here a technical term of Christian doctrine, and must not be confused with the ordinary use of 'person' for an individual.) But by no means all references to Spirit or spirit in the New Testament (let alone the Old) are as specific or clear-cut as that, and it would be absurd to try to squeeze them into a doctrinal mould which they do not fit. Often 'spirit' seems to mean simply 'God, present and active'; and even 'the Holy Spirit' frequently seems to mean something much less specific than the third 'person' of the Trinity. Besides, 'spirit' is sometimes an aspect of human nature, and one can speak of 'my spirit'. Conversely, 'spirit' is not the only word for 'God as present and active'. There are metaphors and symbols and surrogates such as 'the glory of God', 'the name of God', 'the hand, the finger, and the face of God', and so forth. In charismatic circles today, the Spirit of God is a dominant theme; but would it gravely misrepresent the reality if, instead, one spoke of the presence of God in Jesus Christ, or of God powerfully at work through Jesus Christ? The beautiful hymn, 'Spirit of mercy, truth, and love. . . .', though addressed to the Spirit, might almost as well be addressed simply to God, for anything that is quite specific or distinctive in it. With references to Jesus Christ, it is a different matter. No distinctively Christian statement could fail, sooner or later, to mention Jesus Christ, for it is through him, as Christians believe, that new life and a new experience of God's presence are attained. But it might be possible to give an adequate account of a Christian experience—even of a 'charismatic' kind—without expressly naming the Spirit. Thus, 'Spirit' certainly can be used, and in certain circumstances is used, simply for divine presence or divine activity; and for this there are other terms that, in some contexts, would serve equally well. As a random example from modern usage, the song quoted at the beginning of I. M. Fraser's *The Fire Runs* (just referred to) uses 'the Holy Spirit' and 'Jesus' almost interchangeably. Incidentally, it also provides further illustrations of that modern use of the fire metaphor:

> Like fireworks lighting up the night
> the Holy Spirit came:
> dejected Christians felt the touch
> of living fronds of flame—
> and suddenly the world was young
> and nothing looked the same.

> for Jesus' nearness gave them heart
> to venture, come what would:
> the love of Jesus bade them share
> their house, possessions, food:
> the mind of Jesus gave them speech
> that all men understood.

This is the Spirit who, today,
new daring will inspire
and common folk are given gifts
to change the world entire:
the sparks which flew at Pentecost
started a forest fire.

Similarly, in the 'Series III' Order of Holy Communion, Anglicans hear the celebrant say '*The Lord* is here', and respond '*His Spirit* is with us'.

However, this does not alter the fact that there are distinctively Christian experiences of the presence and power of God for which there is no term so appropriate as 'Spirit', provided it is made clear that Jesus Christ himself conditions the experience. One may test this appropriateness by taking phrases from the New Testament in which 'spirit' occurs, and seeing how many of them would carry exactly the same meaning if some other word were used. Characteristically Christian experiences and insights have led to highly specialised applications of the word 'spirit'. And this is a challenge to look beneath the surface and ask what controls the usage. This book attempts to do this within the limits of the series to which it belongs, and to open up the great subject of the understanding of Spirit in Christian traditions.

II.   The Spirit of God and the spirit of man

ALMOST wherever one starts, the discussion of Christian experience leads without much delay to some question about the Spirit of God. One might do worse than start by reflecting that English conventions often force a decision as to when to use a capital S for Spirit, indicating it as divine, and when to spell it with a small initial. Ancient Greek manuscripts did not make such a distinction. Modern German usually spells all nouns with a capital initial anyway. But the English translator of the New Testament, if he follows ordinary convention, has to make a choice; and the predicament in which this often lands him is itself instructive.

However, perhaps it will be more profitable to introduce the theme of spirit and Spirit, human and divine, by comparing certain phrases in Psalm 51, from the Old Testament, with a passage in 1 Cor. 2, from the New. There are merits in this comparison. It illustrates the important conviction that there is a certain kinship between God and man—between Spirit and spirit. 'The Hebrew-Jewish thought', wrote H. W. Robinson[1], 'had found its own way of relating man to God, and of conceiving God as actively present in human consciousness and life'. 'Spirit' is one of the words used in Hebrew and Jewish literature, alongside such terms as 'Word' and 'Wisdom', to help the mind to bridge the gap between a transcendent God and his creation. It is a mediating word; and the fact that in both Ps. 51 and 1 Cor. 2 words for 'spirit' are used with reference both to God and to man is itself significant. But comparison of Ps. 51 and 1 Cor. 2 is further instructive, because it illustrates the new and distinctive dimension given to the word by the Christian situation.

Four times the Hebrew word *ruach* is used in Ps. 51. (The

translators of the Old Testament in the New English Bible use
a small 's' even for the divine Spirit.) Verses 10 to 12 read:

> Create a pure heart in me, O God,
> and give me a new and steadfast spirit;
> do not drive me from thy presence
> or take thy holy spirit from me;
> revive in me the joy of thy deliverance
> and grant me a willing spirit to uphold me.

Verse 17 reads:

> My sacrifice, O God, is a broken spirit;
> a wounded heart, O God, thou wilt not despise.

What is specially significant here, for the present purpose, is
that the psalmist sees *ruach*, spirit, as within him and as part of
him—almost as an attitude or character; and yet, the same
word stands for something that belongs to God and may even
be taken away by God. This suggests that even what may be
called a man's spirit is not necessarily his own, or inherently
his: it may be God's Spirit in him.

Incidentally, this is one of only two passages in the entire
Old Testament where spirit is called 'holy'. The other passage
is Isa. 63.10 f. ('. . . they . . . grieved his holy spirit . . . Where is
he who put within him [i.e. Moses] his holy spirit . . . ?'). Both
passages may belong to a late stage in the Old Testament
period. Still later, subsequently to the Old Testament period,
the phrase 'holy spirit' became more common. In another
chapter of this book it will be appropriate to consider why the
usage became more common at that stage. But at present what
concerns us is not the use of the adjective 'holy' but the ambi-
valence of 'spirit' as man's spirit and yet also God's Spirit, on
loan, as one might almost say, to man from God.

For in 1 Cor. 2 also, *pneuma*, the Greek equivalent of the
Hebrew *ruach*, is used with reference both to God and man.
Verses 9 to 16 read:

> 'But, in the words of Scripture, "Things beyond our seeing,
> things beyond our hearing, things beyond our imagining, all
> prepared by God for those who love him", these it is that

God has revealed to us through the Spirit.

'For the Spirit explores everything, even the depths of God's own nature. Among men, who knows what a man is but the man's own spirit within him? In the same way, only the Spirit of God knows what God is. This is the Spirit we have received from God, and not the spirit of the world, so that we may know all that God of his own grace gives us; and, because we are interpreting spiritual truths to those who have the Spirit, we speak of these gifts of God in words found for us not by our human wisdom but by the Spirit. A man who is unspiritual refuses what belongs to the Spirit of God; it is folly to him; he cannot grasp it, because it needs to be judged in the light of the Spirit. A man gifted with the Spirit can judge the worth of everything, but is not himself subject to judgement by his fellow-men. For (in the words of Scripture) "who knows the mind of the Lord? Who can advise him?" We, however, possess the mind of Christ.'

Paul does not often use *pneuma*, 'spirit', to denote an aspect of man. More usually, he uses *nous*, which is often translated 'mind', to denote that side (so to speak) of a man which is open to the divine.[2] It is noteworthy however, that in Ps. 51, *ruach*, 'spirit', is twice used in parallel with 'heart' (Hebrew *leb*, which is often near to meaning 'intelligence' or 'mind'). This is a common phenomenon in the Old Testament. 'Spirit' and 'heart' are frequently used in parallel clauses as virtual synonyms to denote human impulses or intentions. (Random examples are in Exod. 35.21 and Ezek. 18.31.) Here, in 1 Cor. 2, Paul, following this analogy rather than his usual habit, dares to express the affinity between God's Spirit and something in man by using the single word *pneuma* for both. Like the psalmist, he seems to be conscious of a kinship between the divine and the human. He speaks of the Spirit of God and the spirit of man, and treats the two as analogous to one another. Ancient Greek and Hebrew, as has already been remarked, did not use different sizes of initial letters—capital and small; but the Christian translator into English now, with his custom of using a capital letter for a proper name and for the divine, is beset by the difficulty already referred to. He has to decide when to use a capital letter. Paul seems to be giving an account of what happens when God reveals himself to human consciousness—when revelation occurs. In revelation, Paul seems to say, the divine Spirit touches (or even coincides or coalesces with?) man's spirit. God's self-consciousness, if one may venture the term, becomes a man's self-consciousness, so that a man is enabled to think God's thoughts after him. As G. S. Hendry puts it, '. . . the Spirit is God knowing himself, and to receive the Spirit is to participate in that knowledge'.[3] Only so can any inkling of the hidden mysteries of the divine be imparted to a human person. The analogy is expressed by the parallel uses of *pneuma* in exactly the same way in another important passage, namely Rom. 8.16 : '. . . the Spirit of God joins with our spirit in testifying that we are God's children'.[4]

This observation that only God's Spirit is able to search the mysteries of God and to communicate them crops up more than once in Jewish literature just subsequent to the Old Testament period. For example:

> 'With difficulty we guess even at things on earth, and laboriously find out what lies before our feet; and who has ever traced out what is in heaven? Who ever learnt to know thy purposes, unless thou hadst given him wisdom and sent thy holy spirit down from heaven on high?
>
> Wisdom of Solomon 9.16f.

And in this, from the story of Judith, the implications are the same, although the Spirit is not mentioned and revelation is not directly in view:

> 'You cannot plumb the depths of the human heart or understand the way a man's mind works; how then can you fathom man's Maker? How can you know God's mind, and grasp his thought?'
>
> Judith 8.14.

One might say in the picture-language of St John's Gospel, that the well is deep and that, unless God supplies it, there is no bucket (John 4.11).

Thus, if there is to be enlightenment and insight, the two spirits have to come together—the Spirit of God and the spirit of

man—, as in Rom. 8.16 and 1 Cor. 2.10 ff. But in the latter
passage, Paul reverts to his normal usage within a few verses.
Mostly, as has just been observed, he uses *nous*, 'mind', for that
aspect of a man that can respond to God's approach; and he
does so at the end of this chapter. But not without introducing
a startling and dramatic reference to Jesus Christ. He quotes
from Isa. 40, which is part of that section of the Book of Isaiah
that is usually assigned to the period of the Babylonian exile in
the sixth century BC and called 'II-Isaiah'. In Isa. 40 the monotheistic poet-prophet speaks of the sole, inviolable majesty of
the one true God: Who, he asks in verse 13, can know his mind
or presume to instruct him? This same passage is used again by
Paul with magnificent effect in Rom. 11.33 ff., where Paul
emphasizes the unsearchable depths of God's secrets. But
here, in 1 Cor. 2, he uses it in connexion with the revealing of
those mysteries. Using (as in Rom. 11) a Greek version in
which *nous*, 'mind', occurs (although the original Hebrew in
fact has *ruach*, the ordinary word for Spirit), Paul quotes:

'Who knows the mind of the Lord?
Who can advise him?'

But, for Christians, 'the LORD' (God) in Old Testament Scripture was virtually interchangeable with 'the Lord' (Christ) of
their own experience. Paul can therefore add: 'But we have the
mind of Christ'. At one stroke he has indicated two tremen-
dous convictions that lie at the heart of Christian faith. First,
that God's sole majesty remains undiminished by the position
which Christians find the living Christ to occupy. The mind of
Christ is not a second divine entity alongside that of the one
God: it is, somehow, identical with God's mind. And, secondly, that it is possible for Christians to become possessed of this
mind of Christ: to that extent at least, a man is *capax dei*, able
to receive God. But for the Christian it is through Christ that
this capacity is realized and through Christ that contact is
made between God's Spirit and man's spirit, or man's mind.

It will be for a later chapter to concern itself with the vital
work of the Spirit in instructing and guiding to right
decisions—revealing the will of God as well as his nature. For
the moment, comparison of Ps. 51 and 1 Cor. 2 has shown that

Hebrew and Christian monotheism, for all its recognition of God's transcendence and majesty, tolerated—indeed, required—the recognition of an analogy between God's 'self-knowledge' and man's, between God's Spirit and man's spirit. It has shown that revelation—the communication by God to man of that which initially only God can know—takes place, if at all, by contact between God and man on the level of that aspect of a human personality that may be called spirit. Yet also it has shown that there is a certain independence attributed to man. God's Spirit is not forced upon him. He has the capacity for choice. Perhaps, as will be seen in other passages to be considered later, man may even be said, after all, in a sense, to have a spirit of his own, as a permanent aspect of human personality as such, whether or not the person is religious or conscious of God. And finally, the comparison of 1 Cor. 2 with Ps. 51 has thrown into high relief the way in which Christian understanding goes beyond that of the Hebrew Scriptures and Judaism: the belief that Jesus Christ is supremely the Mediator between God and man. To have the mind of the Lord Christ is, in some measure, to have the mind of the LORD God, which is inaccessible without some such Mediator. It is in Christ supremely that the self-consciousness of God and the self-consciousness of man are found as one; and it is through Christ, himself man, that a human person may most fully enter into divine understanding. One is reminded of the mediation of God through Jesus implied in the so-called 'exultation passage', shared substantially by Matthew and Luke (the term 'exultation' is drawn from the Lucan version—'Jesus exulted in the Holy Spirit'):

> 'At that time Jesus spoke these words: "I thank thee, Father, Lord of heaven and earth, for hiding these things from the learned and wise, and revealing them to the simple. Yes, Father, such was thy choice. Everything is entrusted to me by my Father; and no one knows the Son but the Father, and no one knows the Father but the Son and those to whom the Son may choose to reveal him."'
>
> Matt. 11.25–27 (cf. Luke 10.21 f.)

Matthew's version continues with words reminiscent of a

passage in one of the Wisdom books of the Apocrypha, Ecclesiasticus (or the Wisdom of Ben Sirach). In Matt. 11.28–30, the words of Jesus continue thus:

> 'Come to me, all whose work is hard, whose load is heavy; and I will give you relief. Bend your necks to my yoke, and learn from me, for I am gentle and humble-hearted; and your souls will find relief. For my yoke is good to bear, my load is light'.

In Ecclesiasticus 51.23 ff., Wisdom is heard to speak words such as these:

> 'Come to me, you who need instruction,
> and lodge in my house of learning . . .
> I have made my proclamation:
> "Buy for yourselves without money,
> bend your neck to the yoke, . . ."'

The analogy reminds us that Jesus was seen by Christians to perform functions sometimes attributed by Judaism to the Wisdom of God. No wonder, then, that when St Paul found something of God's mysteries revealed in his self-consciousness he spoke of having the mind of Christ.

The use of words for 'spirit' in these passages from the Old and New Testaments has thus proved illuminating. It turns out to be a useful word when monotheism is struggling to formulate both the transcendent aloneness of God and yet also, paradoxically, his accessibility to man. It is a word which is acceptable, too, to a view of man characteristic of theism, namely a view that sees him as imperfect and frail and mortal and utterly dependent on God, and yet as so constituted that he can receive God as no other created being can.

It was observed earlier that religious experience could sometimes be described without resort to the word 'spirit'. And yet, already it is becoming clear that the language of religion would be greatly impoverished without so versatile and so pregnant a word. Sometimes other words will do, and may even do better than 'spirit', to describe the immanence of the transcendent God: God's Word, his Wisdom, and his Name are among such words. But 'spirit' performs certain special functions which the others do not. To try substituting one of these other words in sentences containing 'spirit' is a way of demonstrating that sometimes it is the only suitable word.

If we return, now, to the question of man's spirit, it is to observe first, that the so-called Manual of Discipline in the Dead Sea Scrolls is also struggling with the problem of expressing God's contact with man, and man's degree of autonomy. There are passages in the Manual[5] where man is described as having within him two spirits—a good spirit and a bad—fighting each other in rivalry for the possession of him. The deeply monotheistic convictions of the writer hold on to the belief that both these spirits alike are created beings, created by God and ultimately subject to him. In this respect, there are parallels in the Old Testament. In less psychological and more 'external' language than that of the Manual, Saul is described, in 1 Sam. 16.14, 23, 18.10, as visited by an evil spirit from the LORD. Similarly, in Judges 9.23, the factions in a feud are ascribed to an evil spirit from God. Thus, in both the Old Testament and the Manual, the evil spirit is no rival god. In the Manual, even the good spirit is not itself the divine Spirit of God. Rather, the two spirits are equivalent to what later Judaism often described as tendencies (the word is *yetser* and occurs already in the Old Testament, e.g. Gen. 8.21) or instincts within a man—the instinct for evil and the instinct for good. The Manual's use seems, in fact, to be an example of one of the looser and more psychological uses of the word 'spirit'. When Paul, however, in a celebrated passage in Galatians, comes near to the same idea of internal conflict within a human person, it is interesting that he contrasts, not two created spirits, but the Spirit of God on one side, and, on the other, 'flesh'—meaning by 'flesh' what we might call 'human frailty surrendered to evil', or just 'selfishness':

> '. . . if you are guided by the Spirit you will not fulfil
> the desires of your lower nature [literally, flesh].
> That nature sets its desires against the Spirit, while
> the Spirit fights against it. They are in conflict
> with one another . . .'   Gal. 5.16 f.

Thus Paul preserves the idea that it is God's own Spirit,

mediated by Jesus Christ, that *impinges* for good on the human personality.

Comparable to the idea of the evil spirit in the Dead Sea Scrolls is the conception of 'possession'. The Synoptic Gospels and the Acts assume that unclean spirits enter and possess human beings, and Jesus and his disciples are represented as exercising a ministry of exorcism. Only in a few places elsewhere in the New Testament is there reference to evil spirits (with varying degrees of certainty, in 1 Tim. 4.1, 1 Pet. 3.19, and Rev. 16.13 f., 18.2), and it is difficult to conceive of possession *by individual demons* as compatible with any acceptable view of human personality today. This is not at all to deny the reality of evil or the fact that a human being may be possessed and dominated by it. It is clear that the release of such victims from the grip of evil was an important aspect of the ministry of Jesus and of others, both within his circle and beyond it. (For the latter, significant passages are Luke 9.49 f., 11.19 (Matt. 12.27), Acts 19.13 ff.). But the invasion of a person by one or more of a number of *individual disembodied evil personalities* is another matter. This 'individualised' conception of evil beings seems to have been a current way, accepted by Jesus himself, of visualising the sinister reality of the domination of a human personality by evil.

Here let it be said again that there can be no serious Christian who does not believe that the ministry of Jesus released countless victims from evil, and who does not still feel the urgent need to pray to God for the release of himself and of others from the grip of evil in various forms. But there are those who cannot with conviction subscribe to the practice of exorcism in our own day, if it means assuming that this evil, conceived of as individual spirits or demons invading persons, should be directly addressed and commanded to depart. This latter practice, however well established in biblical days, seems to be no necessary part of intercession with God for the release of those who are in the grip of evil. Therefore, to question the practice of exorcism, in this literal sense of addressing the spirits and commanding them, in the name of God, to depart, is in no way to question the reality and tyranny of evil, or to deny the power of God to release its victims.[6] Again, scepticism about the notion that a person may be possessed by an individual evil spirit is perfectly compatible with a deep conviction that the Spirit of God can enter and possess a person. For the Spirit of God is not divisible into a host of individual spirits (not even Rev. 1.4, with its reference to the seven spirits before the throne of God can mean that!); neither does the Spirit of God 'possess' a person in the sense of tyrannizing him or overriding his or her personality. Rather, the Spirit 'enters' or 'controls' the person in a fully personal relationship and in such a way as to liberate and enrich and bring to the full stature of personhood.

But we are still left with the teasing question whether or not it is realistic to speak of spirit as a necessary and inalienable aspect simply of a human being as such. Passages such as Ps. 51 and 1 Cor. 2 make it seem that, if man has a spirit, it is only on loan from God. Does it make sense, then, to speak of the spirit of someone who makes no conscious response to God? The fact seems to be that 'spirit' is an extremely versatile word, and resists any attempt to force it into a rigid or systematized meaning. Quite apart from the fact that 'spirit' sometimes means simply 'breath'—that which shows an animal to be alive—, the Greek *pneuma* comes, in some places, very near to being synonymous with a man's self, his person: it is like *nephesh* in Hebrew, which, though it can mean 'soul', often means simply 'oneself'. The ancient liturgical salutation, 'The Lord be with you', is replied to, in the idiom of the seventeenth century Book of Common Prayer, by 'And with thy spirit'; but a modern liturgy is perfectly correct if it makes the reply 'And also with you', for the spirit (in such contexts) is the self. In the story of Ruth in the Old Testament, there is a 'you' symmetrically in both salutation and response: Boaz salutes the labourers reaping his field with 'The LORD be with you', and they reply 'The LORD bless you' (Ruth 2.4). Incidentally, the Old Testament also contains the striking phrase by which God is described as 'the God of the spirits of all mankind' (literally, 'all flesh') (Num. 16.22, 27.15), implying that 'spirit' is an aspect of every person.[7] And certainly Paul thinks of human beings as having an innate capacity to recognize and receive God, and therefore as responsible to him. Broadly speaking it is true to the general tenor of biblical thinking to say that there is, in each individual, an aspect of the personality (call it *nous*, 'mind', or *pneuma*, 'spirit') which is capable of responding to the divine. If, through this 'gate' (so to speak) the Spirit of God is admitted, then the whole person becomes 'spiritual'. But if a person allows his instincts, his 'flesh' (though in itself not evil but neutral), to become the bridge-head for an invasion by sin, then the whole person becomes dominated by selfishness and remains merely animal. Even if he has an aspect that can be called 'spirit', which has the potentiality of becoming fully 'spiritual', it will get nowhere: the person remains no more than physically alive—animated simply, or animal, like any other living creature. Only if he lets in God's Spirit will he become a 'spiritual' person and have life in the full sense— eternal life. Thus Spirit must impinge on spirit, if the 'body' is to become spiritual—that is, become a 'body' capable of life with God. This is what seems to be reflected in Rom. 8.5–11, and 1 Cor. 15.44–58.

Perhaps this is a suitable point at which to revert briefly to the matter, referred to in the introductory chapter, of the limitation of the scope of the words for 'spirit' in the Bible. The vague, generalised use of 'spirit' prevalent in much religious talk often includes its application to the work of creation and of the maintaining of the universe. In such 'cosmic' talk, 'spirit' is thought of as God's instrument for creation, and as permeating created things. Such a use was not unknown to antiquity. The so-called wisdom of Solomon, perhaps coming just before the Christian era, a Jewish work but written in Greek and much influenced by non-Jewish, Hellenistic philosophies, has passages such as the following extravaganza:

'For in wisdom there is a spirit intelligent and holy, unique in its kind yet made up of many parts, subtle, free-moving, lucid, spotless, clear, invulnerable, loving what is good, eager, unhindered, beneficent, kindly towards men, steadfast, unerring, untouched by care, all-powerful, all-surveying, and permeating all intelligent, pure, and delicate spirits. For wisdom moves more easily than motion itself, she pervades and permeates all things because she is so pure. Like a fine mist she rises from the power of God, a pure effluence from the glory of the Almighty; so nothing defiled can enter into her by stealth. She is the brightness that streams from everlasting light, the flawless mirror of the active power of God and the image of his goodness. She is but one, yet can do everything; herself unchanging, she makes all things new; age after age she enters into holy souls, and makes them God's friends and prophets, for nothing is acceptable to God but the man who makes his home with wisdom. She is more radiant than the sun, and surpasses every constellation; compared with the light of day, she is found to excel; for day gives place to night, but against wisdom no evil can prevail. She spans the world in power from end to end, and orders all things benignly.'

Wisd. 7.22b—8.1.

Admittedly, this is more about personified Wisdom than about spirit; but, in the rather imprecise rhetoric of this passage, spirit seems virtually identified with Wisdom, and the two appear almost synonymous, and much occupied with 'cosmic' activities. Also in the Book of Wisdom are the phrases 'the spirit of the Lord fills the whole earth' (1.7) and 'thy imperishable breath is in them all' (12.1). Again, Judith 16.14 is instructive. It is a reminiscence of Ps. 33.6,

'The LORD's word made the heavens,
all the host of heaven was made at his command.'

But whereas in the Psalm the Hebrew phrase 'spirit' (or 'breath') 'of his lips' is rightly rendered simply by 'command', so that it is an exact parallel to 'word' or 'fiat', in Judith, spirit has become a mediating agent in creation:

'. . . thou didst speak and all things came to be;
thou didst send out thy spirit and it formed them.'

In Philo, *pneuma*, spirit, has cosmic functions, though not as God's agent in creation (this is, in Philo, a function rather of the Word or *Logos*), but simply as the life-principle and cohesive force which comes from God.[8]

But this 'intertestamental' theme is conspicuously rare in the Old Testament. Gen. 1.2, which is usually quoted as the instance, *par excellence*, of the creative activity of spirit, may be otherwise rendered. Instead of 'the spirit of God hovering over the surface of the waters', the right rendering may be 'a mighty wind swept over the surface of the waters'—not spirit of God but almighty wind.[9] The NEB puts the latter in its text and the former in its margin. If so, Gerard Manley Hopkins' exquisite phrase, though deeply true, must not look for authorisation precisely in Gen. 1.2:

> '. . . the Holy Ghost over the bent
> World broods with warm breast and with ah! bright
> wings.'

Less eloquently, he was anticipated by much early exegesis of Gen. 1.2.[10] But the fact remains that the only clear instance in the Old Testament itself of the spirit as a creative force is in Job 33.4, '. . . the spirit of God made me', though even this goes on 'and the breath of the Almighty gave me life', where 'breath' is clearly not actually creative in the sense of making the substance of a thing but life-giving in the sense of animating it when made. Spirit or breath in this sense—as that which brings to life creatures already made by God—is commoner. This meaning occurs, for instance, in Gen. 6.17, 7.15, Job 27.3, Ps. 104.29, Isa. 42.5, Ezek. 37.5 ff.

Thus, the canonical Scriptures of the Old Testament contain extremely little about a 'cosmic' spirit. Instead, spirit is used chiefly to denote God's powerful action on and within persons, and especially members of his own people; or, occasionally, it means simply the breath of life.

In the New Testament there is even further specialisation. So far from the Spirit's being cosmic in scope (as Christ, the *Logos* of God, is), the Spirit is scarcely mentioned except as among Christians and as the agent of the 'new creation'—the bringing persons to new life in Christ. St Luke's infancy narratives mention Spirit in connection with John the Baptist's circle and the family of Jesus (Luke 1.15, 41, 67, 80 (?), 2.25–27); and both Luke and Matthew, of course, speak of the Spirit in connection with the virginal conception—the nearest that the

New Testament comes to the idea of the Creator Spirit (but can even this be strictly called 'creation'?). Otherwise, Spirit is confined to the Church and the 'new creation'. Christ, as God's Wisdom and Word, has cosmic functions, but not the Spirit.

This looks at first like gross exclusivism, and as though the Christian Church had become narrow and closed in on itself and had forgotten the mighty doctrine of God as Creator and as penetrating the whole of his creation. But this is not really the case; for two reasons. First, (not to mention the cosmic scope of Christ) it is precisely the Holy Spirit that activates the evangelistic work of Christians. If the Holy Spirit is recognised in Christians alone, it is certainly not in order to make them a closed circle. On the contrary, the effect is to open them, indefinitely and constantly, to what is outside and beyond them, and to send them out into the world with responsible concern for everybody.

Secondly, of course, it does not mean that the New Testament writers were not aware of God's activity in all men everywhere and throughout the length and breadth of all creation, or were not interested in this. It is wrong to suppose that the Bible shows no interest in the glories of God's hand both in Nature and in Art.[11] It only means that the New Testament writers, and in large measure the Old Testament writers also, found the term 'Spirit' less appropriate for describing the divine activity outside those who consciously respond to God and outside human kind, than certain other terms. It has been observed that 'the Holy Spirit came into the Christian Theology, through the bifurcation of the doctrine of Divine Wisdom, which on the one side, became the Logos, and on the other the Holy Ghost'.[12] God's Wisdom, God's utterance, his creative fiat—these and other terms describe God's work in the universe and in mankind generally; and it is very remarkable that, in the New Testament, it is Christ who is identified with this Wisdom and Word of God and is seen as active in creation. But Spirit comes to be, as it were, specialised and related rather to 'the new creation', the sanctifying of the people of God. If the Spirit means God immanent in a human life, and especially in a life that is consciously dedicated to him, it is

Christ who, in Christian parlance, is God immanent in the whole universe and is God's medium in the work of creation.

All this is not to say that it is illegitimate to use the term 'Spirit' in the broad and generalised way that is now common—provided the user knows what he is doing. It is extremely difficult to avoid using 'inspiration' (which is a 'spirit' word) to describe the genius of creative artistry, no matter where it occurs. But it may be that the rather surprising specialisation of the use of 'spirit' in the Bible, and particularly in the New Testament, points to something important; and the fact that the cosmic functions are attributed to Christ and associated with 'Word' (*Logos*) rather than with Spirit may be a theological pointer to something distinctive in the Christian understanding of incarnation.

III. The Holy Spirit in the New Testament

Holy

WHY *Holy* Spirit? In the Old Testament, as we have seen, the use of the word 'holy' to characterise spirit is exceptional. The only instances are Ps. 51.11 and Isa. 63.10f. In Jewish literature subsequent to the Old Testament period, the use of 'holy spirit' (or 'Holy Spirit'?) grows in frequency, though mainly in only one connection, namely, the activity of revelation, whether through scripture or directly to the consciousness of godly persons.[1] The chief exception to this limitation of reference is in the Dead Sea Scrolls, where 'Holy Spirit' is used in a wide variety of contexts.[2] And then, in the New Testament and other Christian writings, 'Holy Spirit' or 'the Holy Spirit' suddenly becomes very frequent. Indeed, it is normal in the New Testament for the adjective 'holy' to be attached to 'Spirit'.

It may be that the increasing application of the adjective 'holy' after the Old Testament period is due merely to a reverential avoidance of the divine name,[3] or is even a matter simply of idiom and vogue rather than carrying any very pronounced theological significance. In the same way, one may trace quite arbitrary fluctuations of idiom in English writing. You might date and locate novels (to take a trivial example at random) according to whether they said 'motor car', 'motor', 'car', 'automobile', or 'auto'. But it is tempting to conjecture that, in the case of 'Holy Spirit', it was more than fashion. Perhaps there was a theological reason. Perhaps the term 'Holy Spirit' was felt to be peculiarly appropriate among religious groups whose members called themselves 'holy ones'. In the Old Testament and other Jewish literature, 'holy ones' (literally 'holies', the adjective 'holy' being used as a noun, to denote a holy being) usually means angels or other supernatural beings. On the rare occasions when it denotes human beings, it seems to be in special circles—for instance, the ultra-orthodox, loyalist Jews of the Maccabaean period probably referred to in Dan. 7:18ff. as 'the saints (i.e. the holy ones) of the Most High'; or the members of the Dead Sea Sect, who were specially aware of being 'dedicated ones', persons wholly made over to God, in contrast to a corrupt and worldly hierarchy at Jerusalem.[4] And similarly, the Christians of the New Testament, who began as a sect of Judaism, called themselves in Greek *hoi hagioi*, 'the dedicated ones', or in Latin *sancti*, 'saints'. This does not mean that they arrogantly thought of themselves as saintly. It only means that they saw themselves called to be intensively dedicated, responsible to God as the very heart of the people of God, the true Israel. And, if so, then 'holy' becomes a specially appropriate description of the Spirit whose presence stamped them as such.[5]

However that may be, 'the Holy Spirit' or 'Holy Spirit' certainly became a current phrase in Christian circles of the New Testament period and after, just as 'the holy ones', that is, 'the dedicated ones', was one of the commonest of the names by which Christians described themselves, thereby signifying that, like the devout Jews of other sects or parties, they believed that their vocation was to be the heart of Israel. ('Christian' was not a self-chosen title: see Acts 11.26, 26.28, 1 Pet. 4.16—the only New Testament occurrences of the word.) But because of its newly established close association with Jesus, the idea of holiness suffered a revolution in meaning. Instead of denoting ritual separation from defilement, it came to denote that intense dedication to the mercy and compassion of God which had led Jesus to touch lepers and fraternise with the more unsavoury members of the community. Holiness was turned inside out: instead of meaning 'holier than thou', it meant 'dedicated for thee'. And it was the Holy Spirit that gave to Christians that 'sanctification' or dedication that enabled them to follow in the steps of a holiness of a 'this worldly' and world-affirming sort.

Trinity[6]

But precisely what is this Spirit—this Spirit called 'Holy' and
given such prominence in the New Testament? The question
brings us face to face with some of the profoundest and subt-
lest of the insights into the nature of God that came with the
Christian era. It confronts us with the roots of trinitarianism.

Is there a trinitarian doctrine of God in the New Testament?
Does 'the Holy Spirit' mean what Christians subsequently
came to call 'the third "Person" of the Trinity'? It has already
been said that it is a gross mistake to try to squeeze New Testament language into the mould of later doctrinal formulations.
But it may be possible, by examining the implications of New
Testament experience, to begin to understand why later gener-
ations came to a trinitarian conception of the unity of God.

The nearest that the New Testament comes to trinitarian
language is, perhaps, in the passages where not just a triple
phrase is employed (for a merely threefold expression is not
necessarily trinitarian) but where 'the Father' and 'the Son' are
used almost as technical terms. They are by no means always
so used. Sometimes in the New Testament they are used non-
technically. The relation between a father and a son is treated
as an analogy or parable for the right relation between God
and his people. It is a familiar fact that the New Testament
portrays a special relation between Jesus as God's 'only Son'
and the Father whom he addresses intimately as 'Abba', 'dear
Father'. All this can still be understood as on the level of analogy or parable. It is possible[7] to interpret phrases such as 'The
Father loves the Son' (John 3.35), or '. . . no one knows the
Son but the Father' (Matt. 11.27) as generalisations, as much
as to say that any father and son (if their relation is good) enjoy
mutual understanding. (If so, 'father' and 'son' should not, in
such passages, be spelt with capital F and S.) But when these
terms are taken out of the immediate context of this analogy,
and used independently, almost as titles—'the Father', 'the
Son'—, then it begins to appear that some kind of eternal relations within the Deity are being hinted at. This is true of the
baptismal formula in Matt. 28.19:

'Go forth therefore and make all nations my disciples;

> baptize men everywhere in the name of the Father and the Son and the Holy Spirit . . . ;'

and of certain passages such as I John 2.22f.[8]:

> 'Who is the liar? Who but he that denies that Jesus is the Christ? He is Antichrist, for he denies both the Father and the Son: to deny the Son is to be without the Father; to acknowledge the Son is to have the Father too.'

There are numerous passages in the New Testament where merely a triple formula, containing words for God, Christ, and the Spirit, appears (1 Cor. 12.4 ff., 2 Cor. 13.13, Eph. 4.1 ff., 2 Thess. 2.13 f., 1 Pet. 1.2, Rev. 1.4 f.); but these are not in themselves necessarily any indication of an awareness of an eternal and necessary threefoldness in the one Godhead. After all, quite outside Christianity, threefold phrases occur in descriptions of the divine. Plato's cosmogony, in his dialogue the *Timaeus*, drew many commentators, from Posidonius in the first century BC to Proclus in the fifth century AD; and these commentators develop various transcendental triads such as 'father, creator, artificer', or 'father, artificer, cosmos', or 'mind, artificer, cosmos';[9] but none of these means a strictly trinitarian interpretation of the Deity. And within the New Testament, threefold phrases are not confined to God, Christ, and Spirit. There is, for instance, 'God, Christ, and the holy angels' (1 Tim. 5.21). Still less significant, in this particular respect, is the so-called 'trishagion'—the 'thrice holy' cry of the seraphim in Isa. 6.3, which is taken up in Rev. 4.8, and, in the so-called 'Apostolic Fathers', in 1 Clement 34.6. Later theology and liturgy saw this as a significant intimation of the threefoldness of the deity. But in Isa. 6 and Rev. 4 it appears to be simply a reverential repetition. No: more significant, probably, than merely threefold formulae is the conviction of an eternal plurality (no matter whether it is dual, triple, or manifold) within the unity of God. What mattered most was that Christians were led by their experience of Jesus Christ, and especially by their conviction that he was absolutely and irreversibly alive beyond his death and was in a special sense one with God, to understand him as himself an eternal, inalienable aspect of the one God of Jewish monotheism. This is more momentous than that they went on to a similar conception of the Spirit. That they did, is, no doubt, important and significant; so it is that Christ came to have cosmic functions attributed to him, whereas the functions of the Spirit were, as we have seen, regarded as within the redeemed community; and so it is, finally, that Christ was believed both to have received and to have bestowed the Spirit. But the most significant new step in theology to which the Christian experience pointed was the recognition that the unity of God was, as it were, in dialogue with itself. It was not a static, monolithic unity—a mere cypher, numerically one. It was a living, pulsating unity, a unity of relationship, the unity between the Father and the Son. Plurality in unity was the supreme revelation. A 'binitarian' conception of God was the pioneer insight. It is important, but of secondary importance, whether it should eventually emerge that the logic of such understanding of unity points to infinite plurality or, at the opposite pole, simply to binity, or, as the Church in fact came to believe, to trinity. This will be further discussed in the next chapter.

It is however, worthwhile to note that Christ and the Spirit are, broadly speaking, distinguished in the New Testament.[10] Attempts are often made virtually to identify the risen Christ, in Paul's writings, with the Spirit. Such a conclusion is sometimes drawn from such phrases as 2 Cor. 3.17 ('the Lord is the Spirit') and 1 Cor. 15.45 ('. . . the last Adam became a life-giving Spirit'). But a good case can be made for finding in 2 Cor. 3.17 a reference, rather, to the LORD God of the story in Exod. 34 which is referred to in this passage.[11] And in 1 Cor. 15.45 the phrase is simply contrasting Christ, 'the ultimate Adam', with the first Adam: if the first Adam was merely *alive*, and was a *creature*, the last Adam, by contrast, was *life-giving* and *spiritual*. This is certainly not cogent evidence for blurring the distinction between Christ and the Spirit[12]; nor, as will be seen shortly, is it, in itself, a statement about the Holy Spirit as life-giving. It seems more precise, therefore, to adopt, as a summary of New Testament tendencies regarding the relation of Christ and Spirit, some such formula as 'God, present as Spirit through Jesus Christ'.

The work of the Spirit

But this brings us back to the place and status of the Spirit in New Testament thought. What is the 'work', what are the activities of the Holy Spirit, and how are they related to the work of Christ?

Inspiration

One important activity of the Spirit will be discussed in a later chapter, namely that of enabling persons to put into words insights into God's character and will—in other words, the gift of prophecy in the widest and deepest sense, or of 'inspiration' (though this is not a word used for it in the New Testament). This, then, may be mentioned here but deferred (see pp. 52 ff. below).

Life-giving

Another function attributed to Spirit in the New Testament is one that is now built into one of our creeds: the Spirit is called the life-giver. Animation, making physically alive, was, of course, associated from very ancient times with spirit in the sense of breath: living creatures were said to have in them the breath or spirit of life (though for this the Hebrew of the Old Testament generally used not *ruach*, 'spirit', but a different word, *neshamah*, 'breath'). But in the New Testament the Spirit is the breath of *new* life—the bringer of eternal life. Nothing could be more important than this new life. It is not, however, so distinctive of the Spirit in particular as might be expected, and it is doubtful whether one should regard it as a particularly significant function of the Spirit as such. Discounting 1 Cor. 15.45, which, as has just been said, is questionably relevant to this theme, the other occurrences are as follows. John 6.63 ('The spirit alone gives life; the flesh is of no avail; the words which I have spoken to you are both spirit and life') apparently identifies the message of Jesus as itself life-giving, and contrasts it (as 'spirit'—small 's') with the externals ('the flesh') which are only the medium through which the life is conveyed. Thus 'spirit' and 'life-giving' both serve as descriptions of the message of Jesus. It is hardly a saying about the function of spirit or Spirit as such. In Rom. 8.11, although it is God who is the subject of the verb 'to make alive', it is through his indwelling Spirit that he does it; and in verses 6 to 13, Spirit (or spirit) is closely associated with life. To that extent, this is a more significant statement, for our purposes, than the saying in St John's Gospel. In 2 Cor. 3.6, however, we are back to something nearer the Johannine theme: the letter of the Law (the Mosaic Law simply as a code or a system, stating God's will but not empowering to do it) can only pronounce judgement and condemn. It is the Spirit—the presence of the living God—that gives life. Here, it is true, it is 'Spirit' with a capital 'S', and the Spirit is indeed the source of life; but it is still (as in the Johannine passage) chiefly in the interests of the contrast between the external and the internal that 'life-giving' is mentioned. Gal. 5.25 must be included here, but only as a possibility. Here *pneuma* is used twice in the dative case: 'If we live *pneumati, pneumati* let us also walk.' The NEB, taking the dative as instrumental, translates, 'If the Spirit is the source of our life, let the Spirit also direct our course' (literally, 'If we live by Spirit, by Spirit let us also walk'). If this is correct, here, indeed, a Christian's true aliveness is attributed to the Spirit. But this cannot be counted as a certain instance of such a thought. The first clause could be rendered, 'If we live *to* the Spirit',[13] which would indicate a life lived for, or in conformity with, the Spirit. Finally, in 1 Pet. 3.18, Jesus himself is said to have been 'made alive in spirit'. But, once again, this is in contrast to 'put to death in flesh'—the same antithesis between spirit and flesh; and, in any case, as will appear later, 'spirit' here probably refers to a spiritual realm, just as 'flesh' denotes a realm or sphere.

Thus, although 'life-giver' is familiar from the so-called Nicene Creed as a designation of the Spirit, the New Testament gives only qualified support to the selection of this function as distinctive of the Spirit. Elsewhere, God and Christ are equally prominent in bestowing life. It must be added, however, that 'rebirth' is attributed to the Spirit, and this is very close to being (newly) made alive. This aspect of

Christian experience will be mentioned at the end of the next paragraph.

Abba!

Meanwhile, a more profound and far-reaching observation is that the Holy Spirit within us puts into action, and sometimes into words, what it means to be a Christian. The Spirit, that is to say, reproduces in Christians the relation of Christ to God as Son to Father. That means that the Spirit is a revolutionary force. The character of Christ is the character of renewed humanity—humanity turned away from self and back to God; and to be under the power of his Spirit causes just such a turning or revolution in each Christian's character.[14] Twice over, Paul says that it is the Spirit that enables Christians to address God with the word 'Abba' (Rom. 8.15, Gal. 4.6). According to Mark 14.36, this is how Christ himself addressed God in his great 'agony', that is, wrestling with temptation, in the Garden of Gethsemane: '"Abba, Father", he said, "all things are possible to thee; take this cup away from me. Yet not what I will, but what thou wilt."' There is no evidence that this particular form of the Aramaic for 'Father' was in use at the time in Jewish idioms of prayer. Jesus seems to have broken away from custom in using this intimate and colloquial form of address (if not specially of young children, at any rate of someone who is very close to his or her father);[15] and it is evidence of the impression it made that, although it does not actually occur in the other Gospels, tradition has preserved this Aramaic word here, transliterated. There is stands, in an otherwise Greek sentence—an alien word, rather like the Greek *Kyrie* in an otherwise English liturgy. It is hard to avoid the conclusion that Jesus really did use the word, and that it was, in such a context, sufficiently new and unusual to be remarked and kept as it stood, transliterated but untranslated, when Aramaic traditions were translated into Greek. Addressing his heavenly Father with exceptional intimacy, Jesus does not, however, take advantage of this familiarity. He uses the 'Abba' address to offer to God his complete obedience. The intimate word conveys not a casual sort of familiarity but the deepest, most trustful reverence. A good case can be made for the view that the Lord's Prayer, the prayer that Jesus taught his disciples, began, in its original form, with the same direct intimacy: not the slightly formal, liturgical 'Our Father in heaven', which has come into all extant versions of the Lord's Prayer, like the 'Our Father, our King' of the Jewish Prayer Book,[16] but simply 'Abba—dear Father'. At any rate, Paul, still retaining the Aramaic word in transliteration, says that it is uttered in Christians by 'a Spirit of adoption' (Rom. 8.15), that is, probably, 'a Spirit that makes us sons' (so the NEB), or by the Spirit of God's Son (Gal. 4.6). This adds up to just what we have already read in 1 Cor. 2—that it is by the Spirit that Christians are enabled to have 'the mind of Christ', to have insight into God's mind, to think God's thoughts after him, and to know that they are members of his family (Rom. 8.16, Eph. 1.17 f.). And all this means not merely knowing with the head, but knowing with the will and the affections. It is by the Spirit, therefore, that Christians are enabled to act as Christians and kill dead all that is contrary to God's will (Rom. 8.13), and that Christ's character begins to be formed in each Christian through the filial relation with God. In John 3.3, nobody can see the kingdom of God unless he is reborn. This rebirth is the Johannine word for this same change of character; and here, too, it is attributed to Spirit: unless a person is born by water and Spirit, he cannot enter the kingdom of God (verse 5). 1 Pet. 1.3 also speaks of new birth, but without immediate allusion to the Spirit:

> 'Praise be to the God and Father of our Lord Jesus Christ, who in his mercy gave us new birth into a living hope by the resurrection of Jesus Christ from the dead!'

Confession of faith, and prayer

If the Spirit enables us to be reborn into God's family and to address him with Christ's own 'Abba!', it is by the Spirit, too, that we can recognize Christ as Lord. The Son of God who does his Father's will even to the length of death on the cross is rightly acclaimed as Lord (Phil. 2.11); and it is the Spirit in us that makes the acclamation for us: the Spirit cries 'Jesus is Lord' (1 Cor. 12.3). Thus, the Holy Spirit is the source of the basic, distinctively Christian perception (Eph. 1.17) and confession; and it is because of the bestowal of the Spirit by Jesus (John 20.22f.), with his commissioning of them, that the apostles become the norm of Christianity. It is in the strength of the Holy Spirit that they bear witness to Christ; and with this goes the responsibility for admitting persons into the fellowship or excluding them from it (John 20.23, cf. Matt. 16.16 ff., 18.15 ff.). But sometimes it is impossible, even with the Spirit's help, to be articulate Christians; and when we are at a loss and can do no more than groan incoherently, the Spirit interprets even the groaning, turning it into prayer to God (Rom. 8.26). Whether or not this is a reference to 'speaking with tongues',[17] the point is the same: it is the indwelling Spirit relating us to God and making contact for us with him. The phrase 'praying in Spirit' (Eph. 6.18, Jude 20) probably means praying in the power or under the control of the Spirit and with the ability given by the Spirit. It is evident that New Testament Christianity was very vividly conscious of this control by the indwelling Spirit—control, but not tyrannical domination. And the Spirit's presence constitutes a solemn responsibility. Each individual and each congregation is likened to a shrine in which the Spirit dwells (1 Cor. 6.19, 3.16), and reminded of the solemn responsibility of keeping that shrine unspoilt by dissension and pure from selfishness.

Conviction

What must be noted next is the function of the Holy Spirit in searching the conscience and convicting. The farewell discourses in St John's Gospel speak of the Spirit as 'the Spirit of truth' (14.17, etc.); and one saying (16.8–11) represents the Spirit as convicting opponents of their untruthfulness and their sin. It is in keeping with this that elsewhere also the Spirit is associated with judgement. The Baptist's announcement that the One who was to come after him would baptize with Spirit and fire (if this is the authentic language) probably refers, as we have already seen, to coming judgement (see above pp. 2f.). The harsh story in Acts 5 about the death of Ananias and Sapphira is concerned with 'lying to the Holy Spirit' (5.3, cf. verses 4, 9). And already, in the Synoptic

Gospels, in accounts of the sayings of Jesus during his ministry, there are those severe sayings about the irreversible consequences of sinning against the Spirit (Matt. 12.31, Mark 3.29, Luke 12.10). What is perhaps intended by this is (in one context) a refusal to face facts, owing to self-interest and pride; or (in another context) a failure to adhere to the truth, owing to self-interest and cowardice. There are three other 'no forgiveness' passages in the New Testament. Two are in the Epistle to the Hebrews. In chapters 6 and 10 there are references to the impossibility of renewal in certain circumstances. The third is in 1 John 5.16 f., where there is reference to a sin that leads to death—a 'mortal' sin—for which there is no guarantee that intercessory prayer will avail. (In Acts 5, already mentioned, deliberate hypocrisy is called lying to the Holy Spirit, and leads to literal death). But of these three only the one in Heb. 10 is actually associated with the Holy Spirit (verse 29 speaks of insulting the gracious Spirit). All these passages have caused great difficulty, heart-searching, and distress. What may one say about them? The passages in Luke, Hebrews, and 1 John all appear to relate to apostasy in persecution, and it is possible that the stringency of their wording is due to the stress and urgency of such situations. It is also in precisely such situations that Christians who trust God are promised the Spirit's help. In Mark 13.11, the disciples are told that the very voice of the Spirit will utter itself in their defence. In Acts 6.10, Stephen is said to have this irresistible force when attacked by his opponents, while they, by contrast, are spoken of as fighting against the Holy Spirit (Acts 7.51). In 1 Pet. 4.14, it is when Christians are under attack that God's glorious Spirit rests upon them. And in Eph. 6.17, the Spirit's sword, which is called 'the word (or utterance) of God', may well mean, similarly, the triumphant witness that God puts on the lips of a confessor when he obeys God. The reference to the unforgivable sin in Matthew, however, seems not to be in a context of apostasy. It relates, rather, to a situation in which, for nothing but partisanship and vested interests, the opponents of Jesus are deliberately attributing to the powers of evil what anybody honest can see to be supremely and obviously good. 'The unforgivable sin is the refusal to recognize the nature of Jesus' authority, for that is to sin against the holy spirit'.[18] So it is that Stephen's persecutors fight against (one might translate it 'collide with') the Holy Spirit (Acts 7.51).

It is understandable that *for as long as* a person deliberately shuts his eyes like this to truth, or *while* he is consciously disloyal to what he believes to be his true allegiance, it is impossible for him to be reconciled with God. And it is intelligible that such attitudes should be described in terms of a person's stance towards the Spirit of God. It is this stance which is described in Isa. 63.10 as 'grieving God's holy Spirit'—a phrase picked up in Eph. 4.30; and the description there of the Holy Spirit as a seal which guarantees the final claiming of his own by God is a further reminder that to 'grieve' the Spirit is to renounce one's membership of the people of God. But it is difficult (and to some, impossible) to believe that there is any sin, however heinous, for which God's forgiveness would not be available *if and when* a true, responsive penitence was shown. That, at least, is reason for believing that to be distressed about the unforgivable sin is evidence that one has not committed it. Peter renounced his Lord, but was forgiven.

Baptism

Membership in the Christian community is brought to a sacramental focus in Christian baptism. Baptism is in the name of Jesus Christ (Matt. 28.19, Acts 2.38, etc.); it brings one into membership in his body, and so into organic relations with other Christians (1 Cor. 12.13); it means a sharing in the obedience of Christ himself as Son of God, in his death and resurrection (Rom. 6.3 ff.); and it is accompanied by the Holy Spirit (Acts 2.38, 1 Cor. 12.13, etc.). This points in a striking way to the distinctiveness of Christianity. The use of a water-rite is not in itself distinctive. There can be scarcely any religion, ancient or modern, which does not make some symbolic use of water: certainly at the time of the New Testament there were plenty such. But here is a striking and radically new nexus of ideas and events: water-Spirit-death-life-sonship; and when one finds that the traditions in the Gospels show us a similar nexus in the life of Jesus, it is hard to resist the conclusion that it is this that gave to Christianity its distinctive use of water. The baptism of Jesus at the hands of John the Baptist is associated with the descent of the Spirit and his consciousness of being the Son of God. The Spirit then causes him to go into the wilderness where this sonship is put to the test. And the cost of this sonship is the cross, and its issue is resurrection. The pattern is precisely the pattern that goes with Christian baptism; but the difference between Christ and Christians is that Christ not only receives the Spirit but bestows it. His own sonship is (it would seem) inherent and unique. The sonship of Christians is derived; it is by adoption, which is brought by the Spirit. 'The Spirit of Jesus' (using the name 'Jesus' alone) is a unique phrase occurring only at Acts 16.7;[19] but it appropriately signalises the close connexion between the Jesus of history and the Spirit of God as experienced through him in the period after the first Easter.

The Pledge

It is for this reason also that, like the Dead Sea Sectarians,[20] but in contrast to some other types of Judaism at the time, Christians saw the presence of the Holy Spirit among them as a pledge that a climax had been reached in God's design and that a future consummation was to be looked for. This Christ-like relation with God, this sonship brought by the Spirit, this beginning of membership in the family of God, was a guarantee that ultimately the process would be completed and God's design for man's glorious destiny would be achieved. Ps. 8 declared man, though frail, to be designed for glory and dominion. In Christ this had already been realized through his absolute self-giving and the absolute life that ensued (Heb. 2.6–9). And in Christians the same pattern began to be implemented by the Spirit. This expectancy attaching to the present manifestations of the Spirit is expressed in many different ways in the New Testament. In Rom. 8.19–21 Paul looks forward to the revealing of the children of God in their glorious freedom—that is, to a time when the meaning will be fully known of that membership in God's family of which the Spirit gives us a foretaste. And Paul sees this as the goal for the entire created world. The full realization of man's true position in the family of God is going to bring the whole groaning, dislocated creation to the satisfaction and fulfilment from which man's original failure in sonship had debarred it. In Rom. 5.12 Adam's disobedience is described as having universal repercussions; and Rom. 8.20 relates it to the whole of creation: 'it [the created universe] was made the victim of frustration'. Admittedly, not all commentators agree that the word rendered 'the created universe' does mean the entire creation, including the non-human or 'Nature', as we call it.[21] Admittedly, too, if this is what is meant, the 'groaning' of Rom. 8.22 and the 'eager expectation' of verse 19 have to be accepted as a daring, poetic personification—just as 'satisfaction' and 'fulfilment' can be applied only metaphorically to 'Nature' or to creation in this sense. (In 2 Cor. 5.2, 4, the groaning is in humankind only.) But it certainly fits well with the story in Gen. 3, where man's disobedience is regarded as involving his environment and affecting it: 'accursed shall be the ground on your account . . .' (Gen. 3.17). So perhaps Paul is here (albeit unconsciously) offering what, in modern terms, might be called a profound theology of the environment—a Christian 'ecology', that is, a theological and Christological interpretation of the interaction of the living creatures in a given environment; and the Spirit, already working in and through men, is instrumental in this ecological readjustment, in so far as the Spirit enables choices and decisions to be made in line with God's will, as by sons working with a father. And so the Spirit is also the pledge of its ultimate completion.

Thus, the Spirit's presence in God's people is a pledge (a deposit or 'downpayment', 2 Cor. 1.22, 5.5, Eph. 1.14), a 'first fruits', the seal of God (2 Cor. 1.22, Eph. 1.13, 4.30): all these metaphors convey the conviction that the presence of the Spirit now is a guarantee of the fulfilment of God's purposes in the end. More than once in the New Testament, appeal is made to the manifest signs of the Spirit's presence, as evidence that those who are addressed really belong to God and may feel confident of the ultimate realization of his destiny for them (2 Cor. 3.18, 1 John 3.24, etc.). In the same way, in the story of Pentecost in Acts 2, Joel's prophecy of the outpouring of spirit is quoted (Acts 2.17 ff.). This seems, in its original context, to

relate only to a period of renewal after a devastating plague of
locusts; but it is here taken up as referring to 'the last days'
(verse 17, a phrase not in Joel). In other words, the endowment
of the company with special gifts is seen as a sign of the beginning of the last act in God's great drama of salvation, just as, in
2 Cor. 3, Paul sees the constant presence of the Spirit as a mark
of a new, post-Mosaic era. Formerly, then, the Spirit was only
for exceptional leaders; now, it is for all who are ready to receive the Spirit. Formerly, the reflected glory waxed and
waned on Moses' face. Now, reflected on the apostle's face
from the Spirit's constant presence, it is a constantly waxing
glory. Ezek. 36.26 had referred to 'a new spirit', promised for
the future. Here is the fulfilment. And even if we no longer
expect a termination of history in the same sense as, perhaps,
men of the New Testament did, the tension between the vertical and the lateral, between the absolute and the relative, between inauguration and completion, between 'the already' and
'the not yet', always remains an authentic characteristic of
Christian life.

Constantly, the activities and presence of the Spirit are seen
as a guarantee that God is at work through Jesus Christ, con-
tinuing and implementing Christ's mission until the final consummation. One signal feature of this was the new outburst of
prophetic inspiration in the early Church. But this will be the
subject of part of a later chapter.

The Paraclete

In St John's Gospel, in the farewell discourses (chapters 14 to
16), the Spirit is several times alluded to as destined to come in
the capacity of a 'Paraclete' (translated in the AV as 'Comforter'). This Greek word corresponds linguistically to the
Latin *advocatus*, 'advocate'; and, although it probably carried
not one but many different associations (like so much in the
Johannine vocabulary), the dominant meaning seems to be
that of a champion or representative—an advocate in a broad
range of activities and in more than a narrowly legal sense.[22]
There are comparable notions of Israel's champions, advo-
cates, guardian angels, and mediators in Jewish literature. The
Spirit is thus seen in the farewell discourses of St John's Gospel

as destined to champion the cause of Christ in the apostles, and, through them, in the world. When Christ is removed from sight, and his disciples have to come to terms with the transitoriness and limitations of his mortal life among them, they will be fortified and consoled by the permanent presence of the Spirit. In this sense, the Spirit takes the place of the visible presence of Jesus. In 1 John 2.1 Christ himself is called a Paraclete (definitely, in that context, an Advocate). The Spirit, then, is 'another Paraclete' (John 14.16). There is even a school of Johannine interpretation which tries to show that the coming of the Spirit may be equated without remainder with the hoped-for return of Christ, thus resolving a future hope into total realisation in the period after the resurrection. But this is an over-simplification. The period after the resurrection cannot for St John's Gospel be equated with the finale of God's salvation drama. What seems to be intended in the Fourth Gospel is not to deny a future consummation in terms of Christ as himself the climax and ultimate 'shape' of human destiny, but to designate the experience of the Spirit as the mode of Christ's continued presence with his people. It is in this sense that John 14.18, where Jesus says 'I am coming to you', should be read.

Mission

In much the same way, the Acts, after the pictorial account of the ascension—the withdrawal of Christ from his disciples' sight—, represents the Spirit as implementing among Christians the mission and message of Jesus. In the Acts, it is by the Spirit that the Church's expansion through evangelism is inspired, directed, and confirmed at every stage, just as in John 20.21f. the sending out of the apostles by the risen Christ is coupled with their endowment with Spirit. So it is in the epistles also: the Spirit accompanies and empowers and authenticates evangelism (Rom. 15.19, 1 Cor. 2.4, 1 Thess. 1.5, Heb. 2.4, 1 Pet. 1.12, etc.). It has been well said that mission is not for the benefit of the Church, as though the Church's aggrandisement were its goal. On the contrary, 'the mission is not at the disposal of the church; both are at the disposal of the Spirit.'[23]

Distinctiveness

It is clear, as one looks back over this review of some of the chief New Testament usages, that the experiences of the Spirit there reflected are experiences of the same Spirit of the same God as the non-Christian Hebrews and Jews knew, but now distinctively conditioned and informed by the knowledge of Jesus Christ, and understood in relation to him. It is not that the Spirit of God is now released from its Hebrew context and made more general. On the contrary, it is given an even more specific 'location' in Jesus. Some commentators thus interpret John 4.21 ff., where it is said that neither in Jerusalem nor on the Samaritan mountain was God to be worshipped, for 'God is Spirit'. 'The point,' says G. S. Hendry,[24] 'is not that locality has ceased to have any relevance to worship . . . The meaning is that the location has been redefined . . .' One might say that the Christian experiences reflected in the New Testament suggest that any authentic experience of God as Spirit, at whatever period and in whatever place, and whether before or after the incarnation, implies Christ as its focal point and consummation. This is how Christians found themselves reinterpreting the Old Testament Scriptures, for this is what 'fulfilment of prophecy', at its deepest level, means.

In the New Testament there is, as we have seen, no uniform treatment of the theme of Spirit. It would be ridiculous and bizarre to try to squeeze every New Testament reference to Spirit into the straitjacket of later doctrinal formulation. But, despite the overlap between the functions of the Spirit and the functions of Christ, there is a perceptible specialization in the usages. There is nothing so specific as in the quaint metaphor of Ignatius of Antioch, the martyr-bishop of the early second century, who calls the Christians at Ephesus 'stones trimmed ready for God to build with, hoisted up by the derrick of Jesus Christ (the Cross) with the Holy Spirit for a cable'.[25] But it is fair to say of the New Testament generally, that, even where 'Spirit' means no more than simply 'God present in and among his people', this is a presence conditioned by and yet distinguishable from the presence of the risen Christ. No messianic figure had been expected by pre-Christian Judaism to bestow the Spirit (although Moses is spoken of as bestowing part of his spirit on others, Num. 11.25, Deut. 34.9), but this is exactly what Christians believed of Christ; and it says something about their understanding of the relation between Christ and Spirit. So completely (one writer points out[26]) has the New Testament writers' understanding of Spirit been shaped by their beliefs about the person of Christ that the Spirit of God can become the Spirit of Christ. Putting it in an exaggerated form, John 7.39 can say that (in a sense) 'Spirit was not' until Christ's death and resurrection. It is understandable then, that expressions of at least a triple shape grew up, with God, Christ, and Spirit in them: the historical facts of Christ and his death and resurrection, which constituted the signal event of God's graciousness and generosity springing from God's eternal love, enabled Christians to participate jointly in the Holy Spirit. That is what seems to be meant by 'the grace' (as it is called) in 2 Cor. 13.13. Its meaning is illuminated by the use of the phrase 'the grace of our Lord Jesus Christ' in 2 Cor. 8.9, which, in that context, evidently means the divine generosity, springing from the love of God, that reached its fullest expression in action with the incarnation—God's deliberate 'impoverishment' of himself in Christ:

> '. . . you know how generous our Lord Jesus Christ has been: he was rich, yet for your sake he became poor, so that through his poverty you might become rich.'

Though Paul does not say so explicitly, that 'impoverishment', also called a 'self-emptying' in Phil. 2.7, is equally God's fulfilling of himself in man—his richest self-expression in the medium of humanity. And by participation in the Holy Spirit, mortal persons may enter into the renewed humanity which is the result of this creative love in Christ. God's initiative; Christ's expression of it in history; the Holy Spirit as the means of entering into it: this is all in 'the grace'.

Flesh and Spirit[27]

There is a further use of the term 'spirit', however, particularly in the Pauline writings, which calls for special note. This is its use in antithesis to 'flesh'. 'Spirit' and 'flesh' are often opposed in the New Testament. For instance, in Rom. 8.5 ff., the attitude or outlook 'of the flesh' is contrasted with that 'of the Spirit'. Or, in Gal. 5.16 ff., flesh and Spirit are said to be at strife with each other, so that a person cannot freely choose what he wants to do. Or again, in 1 Tim. 3.16, Christ is spoken of as shown or manifested 'in flesh' and vindicated 'in Spirit', as also in 1 Pet. 3.18 he was put to death 'in flesh' but made alive 'in spirit'; while, in Heb. 9.14, Christ is said to have offered himself to God 'through eternal Spirit'. It is probably always wrong to interpret such passages in terms merely of a contrast between the material and the immaterial, though this is what is most naturally suggested to a modern reader. It is true that, in Gal. 3.3, Paul castigates the Galatian Christians for trying to complete 'in flesh' or 'by flesh' what they had begun 'in spirit' or 'by spirit'; and these contrasting words in the dative case (used, perhaps, adverbially) are rendered in the NEB as 'the spiritual' and 'the material' respectively. It is true that, more than once, 'flesh' does stand for that which is purely material or external or superficial. But on the whole, biblical writers had little room for a dualism of spirit over against matter. Matter as such and flesh as such were not evil but good: God created matter and 'saw that it was good'; God's very Word became flesh. The New Testament does not countenance the kind of asceticism that disparages the body or the physical functions. Even the Johannine contrast between flesh and spirit (John 3.6, 6.63) is not the same as a contrast between the material and the immaterial. But 'flesh' did stand, in the Old Testament as well as in the New, for what is frail, and transitory and mortal. Warning his hearers not to trust in Egypt's supposed military strength, the prophet in Isa. 31.3 says:

> 'The Egyptians are men, not God,
> their horses are flesh, not spirit.'

'Flesh and blood can never possess the Kingdom of God', says

Paul (1 Cor. 15.50)—meaning that mortal man, by himself and unaided, cannot attain immortality. But because it is weak, flesh easily comes to stand for moral weakness. It is that aspect of a person that is most easily invaded by sin and in which sin most readily establishes a bridge-head (Rom. 7.18). Therefore, sooner or later, the Pauline phrase 'according to flesh', 'in a fleshly way' (*kata sarka*) comes to mean 'in a purely secular way', 'without reference to God', 'self-centredly', 'selfishly'. This is how it is used in 2 Cor. 5.16, which (literally) is:

> 'And so, from now onwards we know nobody according to flesh. Even if we have known Christ according to flesh, yet now we no longer (so) know (him).'

The phrase does not mean that Paul might once have been interested in the historical Jesus but has now ceased to be—any more than it means that he has ceased to know anybody else as a historical person! The *kata sarka* goes not with 'nobody' or with 'Christ', but with 'know', and what is here being denied is not knowledge of a truly historical Christ but a purely secular, man-centred, unspiritual sort of knowing (cf. 2 Cor. 1.17— making plans *kata sarka*). In the same way, the outlook of the flesh, in Rom. 8.5 ff., does not necessarily mean a gross or lustful sensuality. It could apply to the most 'respectable' and refined concerns, insofar as they are not referred to God. In Matt. 16.23, Peter, unwilling to reckon with the cross, is severely rebuked for having a human, not a godly outlook—the verb belongs to the same word-group as that rendered by the 'mind' or 'outlook', whether of the flesh or of the Spirit, in Rom. 8.5 ff.[28]

In contrast, 'according to Spirit' stands for an attitude that takes God into account, puts God first, reckons with the way of the cross. In 1 Cor. 15.44 ff., a spiritual body is contrasted with a merely animal body. This, again, is not intended to denote a contrast between the immaterial and the material. It is simply that an animal body has no life other than the life common to all living creatures. The spiritual body—as distinct from a merely 'animated' or living body—is the body (or self?) attuned to God's will and so to the life of the new age.

Ultimately, therefore, 'flesh' and 'spirit' come to stand for two 'spheres of existence', so to speak, or two 'levels'. Of necessity, Christians, while still in this world, live to some extent in both spheres or on both levels. They are 'in flesh' in a purely physical sense, and, as a result, they are not free from the tug of all the self-interest that belongs in that realm. But yet, they have also been transferred into the new realm of Spirit. The two ages overlap. The 'evil age' from which Christ rescues us is still present (Gal. 1.4). We are inevitably 'in flesh' in a physical and material sense. But we need not, by God's grace, live 'according to flesh'. In 2 Cor. 10.3, Paul explicitly makes this distinction. Literally the words are: '. . . walking in flesh we do not campaign according to flesh'. They are well rendered in the NEB by: 'Weak men we may be, but it is not as such that we fight our battles.' So in Gal. 2.20, Paul speaks of his life 'in flesh'. In Rom. 8.8 f., writing, apparently, with less attention to this particular point, Paul uses 'in flesh', in contrast to 'in Spirit' in exactly the sense (it seems) in which, elsewhere (and, indeed, in Rom. 8.4 f.) he uses 'according to' flesh and Spirit. But it is clear that a distinction can be drawn when necessary between these distinguishable uses with the prepositions 'in' and 'according to' respectively—'in' representing a person's involuntary and inevitable condition, 'according to' representing a stance for which he is responsible.

The use of the word 'spirit' is thus often conditioned by what is contrasted with it; but the contrast is seldom that simply of the immaterial over against the material. The subtle nuances of the context and of the writer's intentions have to be taken into account when we try to interpret it.

IV. Subsequent Doctrinal Developments

THE so-called Nicene Creed (though its origin is disputed, and the creed actually issued by the Council of Nicaea in AD 325 is a shorter one)[1] contains these clauses about the Holy Spirit, following the clauses about the Father and the Son:

'we believe . . . also in the Holy Spirit,
which is Lord,
which makes alive,
which proceeds from the Father
which is worshipped and glorified with the Father and the
    Son,
which spoke through the prophets.'

This, substantially, is what is still printed in the Creed in orders of Holy Communion and elsewhere, in various prayerbooks. What does it imply, and how did it develop? The neuter relative pronoun 'which' is used in the literal translation just given, to represent the Greek. The question in what sense the Holy Spirit should be spoken of as personal will emerge in the discussion.

The formulation of the Christian Church's understanding of the Holy Spirit, which took shape in the two centuries following the New Testament period, was largely derived from and dependent on the formulation, at the same period, of the Church's understanding of Jesus Christ. One might almost say that it was a by-product of Christology, and that a trinitarian interpretation of the unity of God was a by-product of a binitarian interpretation. Indeed, there are times when one is tempted to call the credal statements about the Spirit an afterthought. Says H. Berkhof[2]: 'In the classical creeds, he [the Holy Spirit] is mentioned in one sentence after many sentences

43

about Christ. The following sentences about the church, the forgiveness of sins, etc., can be understood as a description of the Spirit's actions, but he is no longer referred to explicitly'. Similarly, in that ancient hymn, the *gloria in excelsis*, which constitutes a part of many forms of the eucharistic liturgy, there are sections expressing adoration of God and of Christ; but where does the Holy Spirit come in? Only in a parenthesis in a relative clause of the section addressed to Christ: '. . . who, with the Holy Spirit, art (the) most high in the glory of God the Father'. The same is true in the *te Deum*: to the address to Christ it simply adds: 'also the Holy Ghost, the Comforter'.

It looks like an afterthought, and, in a sense, that is what it is. This does not mean that the Spirit of God, whether in the Old Testament or the New or in subsequent Christian or Jewish thought, is ever anything less than awe-inspiring, divine, and mighty. But it does mean that it is not immediately obvious that the Spirit should be understood as an eternal and distinct aspect within the unity of God,—an indispensible factor in a Christian description of God, alongside Christ the eternal *Logos* (Word). It was, in a sense, an afterthought to formulate such an understanding.

Historically, we are told that this formulation first consciously began when the Arian heresy was defeated by the main stream of orthodoxy. Broadly speaking, Arianism, named after Arius, its leader, tried to rationalise the status of Christ and the problem of plurality in unity by regarding him as subordinate to God, as a son is junior to a father, and much as a demigod in Greek mythology was subordinate to Zeus. Christ was divine, Arius allowed, but on a level inferior to the supreme Deity: not eternally existent, but an inferior being. He was God's Son in an almost literal sense, Arius seems to have thought: 'There was,' he said, 'when he was not.' (Not, 'there was a *time* when he was not,' for this would misrepresent Arius as placing the Son's origin within time.[3]) Now there is, indeed, much in the New Testament that reflects a sense of Christ's subordination to God. Instances can be cited such as 1 Cor. 11.3:

'. . . I wish you to understand that, while every man has

Christ for his Head, woman's head is man, as Christ's
Head is God';

1 Cor. 15.28:

'. . . when all things are thus subject to him, then the Son
himself will also be made subordinate to God who made
all things subject to him, and thus God will be all in all';

and John 14.28:
'. . . the Father is greater than I.'

But this is not a subordination of the Arian sort. Christ is not a
numerical addition to God's 'staff', so to speak: he is not
God's *aide de camp*. He is, as the Christian creeds understand
the matter, an eternally distinct aspect of the Deity. The orthodox formula that finally succeeded in safeguarding this against
the inroads of Arius used the celebrated Greek word *homoousios*,[4] 'of identical being', to describe Christ's relation to God:
'of one being with the Father', or 'one in Being with the
Father', as modern versions of the Nicene Creed have it
(meaning 'one with the Father in respect of his "being" or
essence').[5] And although Gibbon and many after him have
mocked at Christians for disputing over a single diph-
thong[6]—*homo-ousios*, 'of the *same* essence', as against *homoi-
ousios*, 'of *similar* essence'—it was, in fact, no trivial belief that
was at stake. The *homoousios* expressed the Church's determi-
nation to safeguard the conviction that Jesus Christ was no
mere demigod.

In subsequent controversy, however, Arius' questions about
the nature and status of the Son came to be applied to the
nature and status of the Spirit, and there were those who predi-
cated of the Holy Spirit the subordination which the main
stream of the Church had denied for the Son. But, again, the
proposal was rejected. The Spirit was declared to be in no way
inferior. Why this insistence? Nothing is easier than to quote
Scripture so as to show that the Spirit is spoken of as divine
and personal. How could it be otherwise, if 'Holy Spirit' means
'God at work among men'? That must mean God personally at
work in relation to persons. But the appeal to Scripture,
though freely made by such writers as Athanasius, Serapion,

and Basil,[7] proves nothing as to the eternal 'being' of the Spirit. It only shows that 'Spirit' is a word for a personal God's personal activity. Neither, as we have seen, do the threefold formulae of New Testament writers, mentioning God, Christ, and Spirit or crying 'Holy!' thrice, prove in themselves that God's unity was viewed as an eternal trinity. The doctrine of trinity in the Godhead's unity is not necessarily reflected in a mere threefoldness of expression. The doctine of trinity means that, just as Christians had reached the conclusion that Christ was eternally one with the Father, as a constituent aspect of the eternal unity and plurality of God, so it was necessary to speak of the Spirit also in the same categories.

So, a fully trinitarian doctrine of God raises difficult questions. It is easier to understand how a doctrine of 'binity' arose. Christ was a vivid personality. He had been known by his contemporaries as a friend and companion. And, if their experience of him, then and subsequently, drove them to see in him not only a historical individual but also an eternal and more than individual reality—'one with God in his being'—, yet this could not obliterate the sense of his distinctness: though one with God, he could never be merged in an undifferentiated way in the unity of God. It must be, it seemed, that God's inviolable unity was, somehow and mysteriously, 'plural'. But why include Spirit in this plurality? 'Spirit' is, after all, only one of several terms denoting divine action or divine intention or (especially) divine immanence—that is, God in his activity within his creation. In a statement about God's activity, 'Word' (or *Logos*) and Wisdom can perform this function; so, in some contexts, can God's 'Name', or his 'hand' or his 'finger'. And Jesus Christ was identified by his followers as that divine Word and Wisdom. Why, then, should it not be natural to identify him also with Spirit, and to stop at a 'binitarian' view?

The Church's main stream refused to stop there. It described the one God as Father, Son, and Spirit. It quite explicitly set the Holy Spirit as a third entity in the same category as Christ the Son in relation to God the Father—that is to say, it described the Spirit, like Christ, as 'one in being', *homoousion*, with the Father. This was set on record at the Council of

Ephesus (AD 431), but had already been voiced by several individuals from Athanasius (*ep. ad Serap.* i. 27) onwards.[8] In effect, though without the use of the *homoousion*, the same
position is expressed in the Nicene Creed:

> '... who, with the Father and the Son together, is wor-
> shipped and glorified ...'

Further, there were attempts to define the relation of the
Spirit to the Son. This led to lamentable dissension, con-
stituting one of the most deplorable chapters in the history of
hair-splitting theology. One formula, called by H. B. Swete
'the doctrine upon which the whole ancient Church was
agreed',[9] described the Holy Spirit as proceeding from the
Father through the Son. A rival formula, however, introduced
in the West, said 'proceeding from the Father and the Son'
(*Filioque* or *et Filio*), and it was explained that this meant 'from
the First "Person" (of the Trinity) and from the Second as
from One Principle and by one spiration'.[10] 'It appealed', said
Swete,[11] 'to the Western mind, which regarded it as completing
the doctrine of a consubstantial Trinity'; but '... the East
viewed it with growing mistrust, which became active hostility
when it was discovered that the *Filioque* had been added to the
Latin Creed.' The East never consented to putting it in their
creed. Their representatives might on rare occasions express a
grudging assent to the phrase *Filioque*, but only as the price for
enlisting a Pope's assistance in extreme danger, and not with
the concurrence of the people as a whole. Such uneasy and in-
sincere concordats were the short-lived Union of Lyons in
1274 and the agreement at the Council of Florence in 1439.[12]
Most recently, in conversations held at Moscow in 1976, the
Anglican-Orthodox Joint Doctrinal Commission debated,
among other things, the '*Filioque*', and the Anglican representatives agreed that it ought not to remain in the so-called
Nicene Creed, in view of the circumstances in which it was
introduced into it. But some of them still wished it to be made
clear that they were not dissociating themselves from the
teaching of Augustine on the 'double procession' of the Holy
Spirit. The Orthodox, on their side, insisted on a distinction
between, on the one hand, the eternal 'procession' of the Holy

Spirit and, on the other hand, the 'sending' of the Holy Spirit into the world within time. In the latter sense, they allowed that the Spirit could be spoken of as sent both by the Father and the Son. (See *Anglican-Orthodox Dialogue* (SPCK 1977), pp. 62ff., 87f.).

In the debates in the early centuries, those who treated the authority of Scripture in a literalistic way were able to find scriptural backing for both formulae—'from the Father and the Son' and 'from the Father through the Son'. In John 14.26, Jesus speaks of the Holy Spirit whom the Father will send in his name, just as, in verse 16, he says, 'I will ask the Father and he will give you another Paraclete.' On the other hand, in John 16.7, the phrase is, 'I will send him to you'; and in 20.22, the risen Christ 'breathes into' the disciples, saying 'Receive Holy Spirit!'. But whatever verses might be quoted for either expression, the debate as to which was the more appropriate was as much concerned with the status of the Son as of the Spirit. In the first place, to describe the Spirit as 'proceeding from' rather than to use some such term as 'given by' was an attempt (surely misconceived and hopeless?) to express a conviction about the special origin of the Spirit: not 'created', certainly; but also not 'begotten', as technical, credal language described the Son; rather, an 'emanation' spontaneously streaming or proceeding from the Deity. The so-called Athanasian Creed (but it is in Latin, not in Athanasius' Greek!) has, of the Spirit, *non factus nec creatus nec genitus est, sed procedens*, 'not made, nor created, nor begotten, but proceeding'.[13] Then, to adopt those Johannine phrases which suggested that the Spirit proceeded from the Father through the Son might suggest a first degree of inferiority for the Son and a second degree of inferiority for the Spirit—a kind of hierarchy of Father, subordinate Son, and still further subordinate Spirit. The alternative (and equally scriptural) phrase representing the Spirit as given equally by Father and Son together was therefore a simultaneous gesture towards the dignity of the Son and of the Spirit. This (apart from political complications, of which there were plenty) is why so much heat was generated in debates over the formula. The *Filioque* ('and from the Son') won the day in the West. The East held almost continuously onto the *per*

Filium ('through the Son'). The dispute continued, up to the time of the final schism; and the recent pronouncement just cited shows that it is still a live issue. G. W. H. Lampe sums up post-Nicene orthodoxy damagingly: 'The Son is God subsisting in the mode of filiation, or begotten, the Spirit is God subsisting in the mode of procession: distinctions which are tautologous and lacking in content. There can be no relations where there are no distinguishable entities to be related and there is but one and the same being.'[14]

To most modern readers such a debate must seem tragically trivial and even more hair-splitting than the subject of Gibbon's jibe. This latter, as we have seen, at least concerned something nearer to the heart of Christology. Nevertheless, the *Filioque* controversy, even if mainly due to political exigencies, bears some witness to the importance attached to defining the status of the Spirit, and shows how decisively the collective voice of Christendom (on both sides of the schism between the East and the West) expressed the conviction that the Spirit was distinct from the Son, and that the Deity must be described in trinitarian terms.

Subsequent thinkers have tried to justify this from outside the formulations of Scripture, by appealing to one analogy or another. St Augustine appealed to what he believed was evident in a human individual. Self-consciousness, that distinctive character of human personality, implies an internal dialogue, certainly. But if that accounts for only two participating factors, there is a third factor, namely the relationship, the love between the two.[15] In modern times, R. C. Moberly distinguished between the man as he really is in himself, himself as projected into conditions of visibleness, and the echo or image of himself which comes back to him from without.[16] Again, the novelist Dorothy Sayers attempted to draw a comparable analogy from the experience of an author. In her book *The Mind of the Maker* (London: Methuen 1942) she observes that the author conceives a 'plot' and characters for a novel. This gives us two factors—the mind of the maker and the concept in the mind. But then, the writing of the novel brings a third entity into existence; and if it is a good novel, this entity may achieve a sort of independence—an existence of its own—

sometimes even taking charge of the writer and leading him or her in directions not originally anticipated.

But '. . . the analysis of any human activity' (said the late C. C. Richardson) 'can never yield a necessary threefoldness',[17] and the trouble with all such rationalisations of trinity is, as he pointed out,[18] that a relationship cannot properly be described as possessing personality. This difficulty is endorsed by the tendency to speak of the Spirit as 'it', and the fact that personal representations of the Spirit were actually avoided, Christian art using the symbol of the dove or rays of light. Certainly the fact that Spirit is the mode by which a personal God is present does not seem, in itself, to necessitate the recognition of Spirit as essentially personal; and especially when, outside the Bible, Spirit is applied specifically to God's creative activities at non-personal levels, it seems gratuitous to insist on using a personal pronoun. Thus, a contemporary writer uses, of the Spirit, the phrase 'he works anonymously through all the processes of creation';[19] but would it not be more realistic to make *God* the subject of such a sentence, and, if using the word 'Spirit' at all, to use it for an impersonal force or agency? Thus, might not the sentence be rewritten as 'he (God) works anonymously by the agency of his Spirit'? Where Spirit is most reasonably spoken of as personal is in precisely the contexts most characteristic of the New Testament. When Spirit is the mode of God's presence in the hearts and minds of his people, then there is a good case for personal language. But this still does not force upon us a third eternal 'Person' (in the technical sense) within the Unity.

Perhaps one ought not to agonize too much over problems of trinity in the description of God. What seems to be clear and striking in Christian experience as reflected by the most authentic evidence for the earliest Christians (and, in so far as the incarnation is a historical event, the earliest evidence is important, being nearest to the origins) is as follows. First, Jesus Christ was found to be not only a historical individual but also a transcendent Being. Christians found themselves speaking of him in a way that has no parallel anywhere else: they found themselves led to speak of him as one with God in his very being, and as, therefore, eternally existent. Yet always he

remained identifiable as Jesus of Nazareth, so that the transcendent Lord assumed a distinct aspect within the Deity. This
leads to the conception of God's 'oneness' as no monolithic
cypher but as a unity that is in dialogue within itself, a 'binitarian' unity. Then, side by side with but distinguishable from
the Christian experience of being 'members of Christ', incorporated in him, was the experience of Christ's character being
imparted to each Christian, and Christ's attitude to God being
reproduced in each Christian. And this, by common consent,
seems to have been best described as the work of the Spirit of
God through Christ, or even as the work of the Spirit of Christ.
Thus, in addition to the establishing of an intrinsic plurality in
the Deity, Christian experience led to the recognition of at
least two distinguishable 'modes' of God's presence with men:
the 'mode', namely, in which Christ was experienced as
Mediator, and Christians found themselves incorporated in
him; and the 'mode' in which the Holy Spirit was found in and
among Christians, interpreting Christ and creating his likeness
in them. It is thus intelligible that the Church came to speak of
God as eternally Father, Son, and Spirit. But threefoldness is,
perhaps, less vital to a Christian conception of God than the
eternal twofoldness of Father and Son.

V.   Inspiration and Incarnation

THOUGHT about the Holy Spirit's activity is sometimes blurred by confusion over the meaning of the words 'inspiration' and 'incarnation' respectively. Incarnation (a Latin term for 'enfleshing') stands, when used technically, for the belief that the divine became human flesh and blood. Admittedly, the form of the word might suggest, rather, that the divine *entered* flesh and thus *inspired* it. But 'incarnation' has come to be a technical term not just for inspiration but for something special—for God's becoming man.

Is this a valid distinction? Does it make a difference if one substitutes '*entered* flesh' for '*became* flesh'? The Spirit of God is thought of as entering and pervading 'flesh and blood', that is, a mortal person, when a person becomes an inspired interpreter of God's message. Is this the same as incarnation or different? And if it is different, wherein lies the difference? Is it a difference of degree only or of kind? Or is that a false antithesis anyway? If Christians believe in the decisive nature of God's expression of himself in Jesus Christ, is this simply because he was supremely and totally inspired, excelling in degree the inspiration of all other prophets? Or is it because in Jesus God's utterance had *become* a man, in a way distinguishable from even the highest degree of inspiration?

One may put the same problem in categories other than that of prophetic inspiration. A cliché often used in Christian circles calls the Church as a whole 'the extension of the incarnation'. Does this imply that incarnation in the case of Jesus was different only in degree from the subsequent indwelling of the power of God in Christians? Is it accurate to use the term 'incarnation' ('enfleshing') to describe the entry, in whatever degree, of the divine into any and every human person who is

52

receptive? And, if so, would not the 'extension' have to be backwards, into the pre-Christian period, as well as forwards? Is not 'the extension of the incarnation' an imprecise expression for the Church's continuation of what was inaugurated once for all by Christ, as God uniquely incarnate? Again, in Christian devotional language, one sometimes hears it said that a Christian or a group of Christians needs to 'become incarnate' in some situation—meaning that they must not stand outside and theorise but must get inside the situation in which they are called to serve, and must be willing to 'get their hands dirty' and to identify themselves with it in its costliness and hazards. It is easy to understand and admire the intention behind such language; but it is imprecise and loose, since people who are already of flesh and blood cannot literally become still further 'enfleshed'. 'Incarnation' cannot strictly be used for mere involvement in circumstances.

Incidentally, it is not accurate, either, to speak of Christ's incarnation in the Eucharist, as though the bread and wine of the Eucharist were exactly analogous to the person of Christ in the incarnation, and as though each consecration were a re-incarnation. 'Incarnation', as technically applied in the case of Jesus Christ, means the becoming a human person—'flesh' in that sense. It does not mean the becoming 'flesh' in the sense, merely, of becoming a material thing—if that even made sense in such a context. And it is one thing to believe that the consecrated elements are means by which the believer may receive Christ's very presence into his life, and another thing to believe that, in those material elements when consecrated, Christ is re-incarnated in a personal sense. It is possible to hold a very 'high' or strong sacramental doctrine of the 'real presence' at the Eucharist[1] without believing this. The invocation of the Holy Spirit at the eucharistic consecration, technically known as the *epiclesis* (the Greek for 'invocation'), may be a prayer for the Spirit to come upon the worshippers—that is, to inspire them to receive God in Jesus Christ. But if it is a prayer that the Spirit may come not only into the worshippers but also into the bread and wine, with the implication that they thereby become that in which Christ is embodied as a person, this implies a conception of the functions of Spirit which is alien to the New

Testament and to the Bible generally. It is claimed that the invocation of the Spirit on the Bread and Cup is attested at least as early as Cyril of Jerusalem (fourth century);[2] but the antiquity of the usage does not necessarily recommend it; and, for all its dignity and beauty, the well known Communion hymn 'Let all mortal flesh keep silence' is questionable when it says:

> 'King of Kings, yet born of Mary,
>   As of old on earth he stood,
>   Lord of lords, *in human vesture*—
>   *In the Body and the Blood* . . .'

'Incarnation', then, as technically used, is a term that re-quires careful application, and its edges should not be allowed to become blurred with 'inspiration'—unless this is done delib-erately and for considered reasons. And there are at least cer-tain strands of New Testament thought which seem to point to something demanding a distinctive term denoting a unique category for which it may well be right to reserve the term 'incarnation'. It is true that the statement, 'the Word became flesh'—that startling climax of the Johannine prologue in John 1.14—follows immediately on a statement (verse 13) that all who receive him are divinely begotten, not by blood, nor by physical desire, nor by human design at all, but by God. On this showing, Christians, in a sense, share Christ's own divine origin: they are 'begotten' by God. But whereas they are already also flesh, the Word *became* flesh. Thus, while it is pos-sible to interpret John 1.13 as a hint that divine 'conception' is a metaphor for something common to all believers (meaning that *spiritually* they are 'reborn'), the Evangelist still does not put the incarnation of the Word (verse 14) in the same category as the birth (or rebirth, either) of any human being. And, in any case, the rest of St John's Gospel notoriously treats Jesus as divine in so special a sense that he is placed in a unique cat-egory—so much so, indeed, that this Gospel comes within an ace of presenting only a 'docetic' (that is, a merely apparent) incarnation, and suggesting a divine Being who is merely dis-guised as a man and has not really become a man.[3] John 10.34–36 (strange though its exegesis of Ps. 82.6 is) seems to draw a distinction between those to whom the message ('Word') of God came, and the one whom God the Father has sanctified and 'sent' into the world:

> 'Is it not written in your own Law, "I said: You are gods"? Those are called gods to whom the word of God was delivered—and Scripture cannot be set aside. Then why do you charge me with blasphemy because I, consecrated and sent into the world by the Father, said, "I am God's son"? . . .'

A unique incarnation, again, is certainly the intention behind the references, in Matthew and Luke, to the conception of Jesus by Mary while a virgin. It seems to be intended, literally and exclusively, that it was from no man, but from the very Spirit of God that the semen came (Matt. 1.18, 20; Luke 1.35). In John, as we have just seen, the reference to begetting is, by contrast, metaphorical and inclusive of Christians as well as Christ, although John safeguards the uniqueness by the words 'became flesh', and by much else in his narrative. Whatever may be made, then, of the tradition of the virginal conception, and whether it be treated as literal and true, literal but legendary, or intended from the first symbolically and not literally, the point (for the present discussion) is that it bears witness to an understanding of Jesus as God incarnate, and not simply as a man inspired—not even if the inspiration were 'plenary'.

The same seems to be intended by the obscure phrase in Col. 2.9, 'in Christ . . . the complete being of the Godhead dwells embodied' (so NEB). Although the adverb rendered 'embodied' (*somatikōs*) is sometimes taken to mean no more than 'in actuality'[4]—that is, in fact and not merely in semblance or symbol—, and although it can hardly be interpreted physically, it does appear to mean that God himself, and not merely some force or power distinguishable from God, is in Christ.[5] If so, the present tense ('dwells') must be explained as due to a consciousness of the risen Christ alive now, yet continuous with Jesus of Nazareth. Perhaps this is comparable to the fact that the writer to the Hebrews alludes to 'the days of Jesus' flesh' (5.7), thus implying identity between the human figure of history and the transcendent Jesus subsequent to 'the days of his flesh', of whom the writer speaks.

All this must not obscure the fact that all the traditions about Jesus do present him as inspired, to a supreme degree. But, even if one did not consider the other marks of uniqueness, this inspiredness of Jesus is more than merely a supreme endowment with Spirit. Jesus is shown as the giver of the Spirit as well as receiving Spirit with uniquefulness. John 1.33 reads:

> '. . . this is he who is to baptize in Holy Spirit';

Acts 2.33:

> '. . . he received the Holy Spirit from the Father, . . . and all that you now see and hear flows from him';

and Eph. 4.7 ff., quoting a version of Ps. 68:

> '. . . each of us has been given his gift, his due portion of Christ's bounty. Therefore Scripture says:
> "He ascended into the heights
> With captives in his train;
> He gave gifts to men."
> . . . And these were his gifts: some to be apostles, some prophets . . .'

Moses, it is true, shares his spirit with others (Num. 11.25) and bestows it on Joshua by the imposition of hands (Deut. 34.9, though contrast Num. 11.17, 25); but, in the main, the great inspired persons of Israel are not able to bestow this inspiration on others. Christ is thus, again, portrayed as even more than supremely inspired.

By no means all theologians of the present day find themselves able to accommodate this absolute distinction between incarnation and inspiration, and there is a noticeable tendency to minimize it, even if, by way of compensation, the degree of inspiration attributed to Christ is allowed to have been 'plenary'. As this book was being written, a considerable furore arose in England through the publication of *The Myth of God Incarnate*.[6] This is a collection of essays by seven writers including Professor John Hick who edits them. Broadly speaking, and in varying degrees, they all reject the language of incarnation as incompatible with a belief in Christ as fully man. In any case, moreover, incarnational language belongs, they maintain, to a framework of thought which is no longer valid. They are ready to affirm Jesus as supremely inspired, and they accept the story of the cross and resurrection as a powerful way of expressing the conviction that God involves himself redemptively in human suffering, but the notion that a pre-existent divine Being became a man is rejected as unacceptable; and the origin of the traditional doctrine of the incarnation is sought in the imaginative embroidering of the facts by early Christians in terms of conceptions of deity which modern man can no longer entertain.

Now, all this is eminently logical and intelligible, and for that very reason has been tried again and again in the past. At any rate in essence it is as old as the rationalists of the last century and the early years of this century. Only a few weeks after *The Myth*, came a symposium on the great German theologian and philosopher, Ernst Troeltsch, who died in 1923; and an essay of his which appears there[7] in translation expresses very much the view represented in *The Myth*, namely, that, although one cannot accept the Christology of the New Testament and the Church Fathers as it stands, one can see in Christ the *symbol* and *centre* of an ideology which has lasting value. Much the same would be true, *mutatis mutandis,* of the so-called Modernist Movement in the Church of England in the early years of this century, following that in the Church of Rome. All this and more was pointed out by the contributors to *The Truth of God Incarnate*,[8] edited by Canon Michael Green and rushed into print as a retort to *The Myth*.

In the end, however, material for a more profound reply may turn out to lie in the learned and difficult book which appeared very shortly before *The Myth*—Professor Christopher Stead's *Divine Substance*.[9] In this he examines in minute detail the history, pre-Christian and Christian, of certain technical Greek words that came to be used in the early Christological controversies to some of which allusion has been made in the preceding chapter; and it may be that a more intimate understanding of precisely why and how the terms were used will point to their continued value and indispensability.

Meanwhile, it may be said that *The Myth* represents an

understandable tendency and that it is difficult—perhaps impossible—to fault the logic of its main assertions: that if we are
determined to hold onto the conviction that Jesus was really a
man and that God is immanent in his creation, not invading it
from outside, we cannot combine this with the idea of a pre-
existent divine Being's becoming a man.

If, then, there are nevertheless reasons, as is here maintained, for still adhering to some form of incarnational Christology and distinguishing between incarnation (in its technical
sense) and inspiration,[10] they lie in the earliest evidence for distinctively Christian experience. If such evidence as we have,
when the sources have been critically sifted, for the character
of Christian experience and of Christian understandings of
Jesus at the origin of the movement is simply not adequately
accounted for by eliminating incarnation, then we may have to
admit inability to make a logical system out of the evidence,
and be content to hold to, or be held by, both ends of the dilemma, confessing a mystery which cannot fully be rationalized
without doing injustice to some part of the evidence. There is,
as has already been said, a way round the difficulty which at
first sounds plausible enough. This is to resort to theories of
the genesis of Christology through imaginative embroidering,
leading, in course of time, to the evolution of lofty conceptions
of Jesus which were not justified by the original event. But such
theories are too often invoked without careful attention to the
facts, and they turn out to be themselves uncommonly like a
tissue of imagination.[11] Actually, the earliest Christology
which can be securely dated, namely, that of the great Pauline
epistles, Galatians, Romans, and 1 and 2 Corinthians, is
already as developed and as 'high' (in the sense that it sees
Jesus as divine and transcendent and uniquely one with God)
as Christologies which, on the 'embroidering' theory, ought
only to be appearing late and at the further end of a long, evol-
utionary sequence.

Thus, while it is tempting to accept plausible, logical theories about Jesus as superbly and supremely inspired but not
God incarnate, they seem to represent an impatient cutting of
the Gordian knot and an evasion of the question, How do you
account for the very early incidence of a Christology which

recognized Jesus as the transcendent Son of God? To ask such a question is not blind conservatism. It is an expression of an anxiety lest so tidy and coherent a view as a merely 'inspirationist' Christology may not be an over-simplification in the light of the phenomena of early Christian experience. One has to ask, How least inadequately may one describe what must have given rise to such phenomena? These phenomena seem to reflect One who cannot adequately be described either in docetic or in adoptionist terms: that is to say, he is neither a god disguised as a man (docetism), nor is he simply a man who was raised to the highest heights of inspiredness (adoptionism). And although it may be impossible to work these observations into a coherent system, it is more realistic to hold them together in a paradoxical statement than to force sense upon them by overlooking some of the phenomena. There is no merit in a paradox: we must always be struggling to resolve it. But we may have to live with a paradox if that is what the data seem persistently to demand.[12] It is a familiar fact that the usually accredited test of a realistic doctrine of Christ is whether it yields a realistic doctrine of salvation. Can an inspired person—even with plenary inspiration—achieve what Christians experience in Christ, when they find in him humanity re-created and the new age beginning to be present? If Christ is authentically experienced as not only a teacher but a Saviour, one who rescues the human will from its self-centredness and, when he is allowed to do it, human society from its warped condition, can it be that he is no more than a supremely inspired person? There is no doubt that mainstream Christianity has always found in Jesus Christ a Saviour and no less—a Creator and not an instructor or example only. Information and example may have a limited effectiveness on individuals, given a will and a capacity to respond. But what if this capacity is diminished and the will is warped and what if something more than individual appeal is needed—something as radical as new creation? Remaking from within by God incarnate seems alone sufficient. This view has been radically questioned; but it is difficult to avoid its force. Berkhof remarks[13] that the idea that the Spirit was incarnate in Jesus— that is, a 'Spirit-Christology'—appears in the immediate sub-

apostolic age, in some of the Christian writers of that period—
the so-called Apostolic Fathers (e.g. in Ignatius' Epistles to the
Ephesians 7.2 and to the Magnesians 15; in 2 Clement 9.5; and
in 'the Shepherd' of Hermas, Similitudes 5.6.5); but that by
about the middle of the second century this had died away, to
be superseded by a 'Logos-Christology', i.e. by a return to the
view-point of the prologue to St John's Gospel. It would
appear that experience shows that a mere 'Spirit-Christology',
for all its reasonableness, proves inadequate.

However that may be, and whether one makes a sharp distinction between incarnation and inspiration or none at all, the
subject of inspiration remains important in any study of the
Spirit, and calls for examination. Prophets constitute the most
obvious example of human persons who are inspired by the
Spirit of God, that is, who are in some sense penetrated by the
Spirit of God so that they utter God's thoughts. In an earlier
chapter, 1 Cor. 2.9 ff. was identified as an account of how revelation takes place by reason of such contact between God's
consciousness and man's; and prophets are those for whom
revelation of this sort is more than ordinarily developed. In the
Old Testament, specific reference to the Spirit in connexion
with prophetic inspiration is not as common as might have
been expected, and some of the passages where it does occur
relate to what seems more like ecstatic 'raving' than prophecy
in the lofty sense which is associated with the great eighth and
seventh century prophets of Israel.[14] Thus, in Num. 11.24–30
there is the strange story of how God took from Moses 'some
of his [i.e. Moses'] own spirit'—that is, apparently, a portion
of his divine gift of inspired leadership and vision—and com-
municated it to seventy chosen men, who all showed the signs
of an ecstatic visitation, including the two who were not in the
presence of Moses at the time. It is, however, noteworthy that
the main purpose of this endowment was not prophecy as
such. It was in order that these men might be capable of
sharing the burden of administration with Moses (verse 17)
particularly that of dealing with complaints. Or, again, Saul,
on his anointing by Samuel, 'catches', as it were, this prophetic
frenzy from a band of prophets (1 Sam. 10.10), just as, later on,
he is visited and overpowered by such frenzy against his will

when pursuing his rival David (1 Sam. 19.23 f.). Perhaps Balaam represents a sort of half-way house between this sort of ecstasy and the higher prophecy (Num. 24.3 f.). At any rate, there is, among the stories of the more lofty prophets of Israel, an occasional reference to the gift of the Spirit. In 1 Kings 22, Micaiah the son of Imlah, daring to utter an adverse prophecy against King Ahab, claims that Zedekiah the son of Chenaanah and the other court prophets who have uttered flattering prophecies have been visited by a lying spirit, sent from Yahweh's court expressly to deceive Ahab and lure him to his ruin (verse 23). In 2 Kings 2.9–15, Elisha receives Elijah's spirit—that is, his endowment as a prophet and a wonderworker—when Elijah is taken up to heaven. In 2 Sam. 23.2, spirit seems to be virtually prophetic inspiration. In Micah 3.8, the prophet appears to associate the courage that he finds to denounce the nation's crime with the Spirit of Yahweh; but the sentence is broken and ungrammatical, and there is doubt about its integrity. The RSV (forcing the sense, despite the ungrammatical Hebrew) translates:

'. . . I am filled with power,
with the Spirit of the LORD,
and with justice and might,
to declare to Jacob his transgression
and to Israel his sin.'

But the NEB text omits 'with the Spirit of the LORD'. The NEB's footnote is not explicit about the difficulty, which is that it is impossible—using the words exactly as they stand there—to bring inside a regular Hebrew construction both 'power' and 'the Spirit'. Hence the suspicion that there has been interpolation. However, the celebrated passage in Joel 2.28 connects the predicted wholesale outpouring of God's spirit with prophecy—'your sons and your daughters shall prophesy' (cf. Acts 2.17—though it is a question whether this 'prophesying' is nearer to the raving frenzy or to the deep insight (the dreams and visions mentioned are no certain guide)). Finally, there are other passages which associate the Spirit of God, if not expressly with prophecy, yet with the sort of ministry that fell to the great prophets. Thus, in Isa. 42.1 (cf.

Matt. 12.18 ff.) God's voice is heard declaring that he has bestowed his spirit on his servant for his ministry of justice; and in Isa. 61.1 f. (cf. Luke 4.18) the speaker claims to have been 'anointed' with the spirit of Yahweh for a ministry of rescue and release.

Prophecy in the limited sense of prediction is also sometimes attributed to Spirit in the Old Testament—for instance, in the case of Joseph (Gen. 41.38) and Daniel (Dan. 4.8). In the Old Testament, however, the presence of the Spirit is signalized also in other ways besides prophecy. Very conspicuously, the Spirit comes upon the warrior leaders of Israel to give them wisdom and strength (Judges 6.34, and onwards)—in Samson's case, sheer muscular strength without much wisdom. Equally Bezalel, the craftsman of the tabernacle, is filled with divine spirit (Exod. 35.31). That this is not specified of Huram, the craftsman of Solomon's temple (2 Ch. 2.13), may be due to the Chronicler's having a different outlook and theology; or it may be a chance of vocabulary. It has to be remembered that, in such contexts, 'wisdom', 'ability', and 'spirit' are almost interchangeable. This is clear when one compares the phrase in Exod. 35.31, about Bezalel's being filled with divine *spirit*, with verse 35 in the same chapter, where Bezalel and a fellow-craftsman, Oholiab, are both described as filled with *ability*. (The NEB uses 'inspire' in this verse to render what is literally 'give or put in the heart'.) Again, whereas spirit is not mentioned in 2 Ch. 2.13, of Huram, in 1 Ch. 28.12 'spirit' is used in the description of David's designs for Solomon's temple—though there the RSV and the NEB may be right in interpreting the phrase to mean that David had 'in mind' all the plans, rather than (as the AV and RV do) rendering it 'by the spirit', as though it meant 'by inspiration'.

It is in later Judaism, outside the canonical Scriptures, that the recognition of inspiration as a prophetic endowment becomes particularly clear. Philo frequently makes explicit the link between prophecy and the Spirit; and Josephus also recognizes it.[15] So, too, 1 Enoch 91.1 has '. . . the word of God calls me and the Spirit is poured out upon me'.[16] And there are examples also in the Targums.[17] In the New Testament, 2 Pet. 1.20 f. expressly claims that it was by the Holy Spirit that the prophets of the past were led. Again, Rev. 22.6 calls God 'the God of the spirits of the prophets', meaning, clearly, that God controls their inspiration. Another significant verse in Revelation is 19.10, which seems (if we follow G. R. Beasley-Murray, who is essentially in accord with G. B. Caird before him)[18] to identify the testimony borne by Jesus himself as 'the concern or burden of the Spirit who inspired prophecy'. It is tempting, alternatively, to make it mean that, wherever there is authentic prophecy, whether in the Old or New Testament, it will be found to bear witness to Jesus. But there is strong evidence for taking 'of Jesus' as a subjective genitive: it is not 'witness to Jesus' but 'the witness borne by Jesus'. It is 'the witness he has borne in his life and teaching, but above all in his death, to God's master plan for defeating the powers of evil by the sacrifice of [i.e. the sacrifice consisting of] loyalty and love . . . It is the word spoken by God and attested by Jesus that the Spirit takes and puts into the mouth of the Christian prophets.'[19] Throughout the Apocalypse, the Seer claims inspiration. He was 'in Spirit' (Rev. 1.10); the messages to the seven Churches claim to be what the Spirit is saying (2.7, etc.); the whole book is safeguarded by divine sanctions (22.18 f.).

Thus, the Christian prophet is, like pre-Christian Jewish prophets, controlled by the Spirit of God, but, in distinction from them, it is the Spirit mediated through Jesus Christ. And the function of Christian prophecy is not only to give expression to the witness of Jesus (Apostles and Evangelists and teachers also do this), but to put into words inspired insights into the will of God. The prophet is an interpreter of the mind of God because the Spirit of God is speaking through him and enabling him to 'have the mind of Christ' (1 Cor. 2.16). This is the ministry described in 1 Cor. 14.29–33. Evidently, at Christian gatherings for worship and mutual edification, there would be some present who were recognized as having this prophetic gift—or, if all had it in some measure, these persons had it more frequently or more clearly. They would, on occasion, speak in God's name—probably specifying the right course of action in the face of some need or problem. But it is significant that they were not accepted blindly as final authorities: the rest of the congregation had to exercise their critical

judgement. There is an unpublished record of a meeting of
Christians a year or two ago, in which a prophet spoke in the
first person in the name of God. The prophecy started 'My
people . . .', and went on to warn them against the demonic
powers of evil in the country and to express fierce disdain and
disgust at their selfish divisions. An observer who was present
has said that it was noticeable that the congregation showed
themselves fully *en rapport* with certain parts of the utterance
and less so with other parts. It was like the Corinthian congregation exercising discrimination (1 Cor. 14.29). Similarly, in
the Acts there are some instances where the Spirit's voice (pre-
sumably through the words of persons specially open to the
Spirit) is accepted and followed, and others when it is respect-
fully listened to but not followed. Thus, in Acts 15.28, the
meeting called to consider the terms on which Gentiles might
be admitted to the Christian community attributes its final res-
olution to the Holy Spirit as well as to the assembly: 'It is the
decision of the Holy Spirit, and our decision . . .'; and in Acts
16.7 'the Spirit of Jesus' (a unique phrase)[20] prevents the evangelists from going in a certain direction. By contrast, in Acts
21.4 Paul refuses to take advice given 'through the Spirit', that
is, as an inspired utterance; and in Acts 21.10 ff. the prophet
Agabus, who, under the influence of the Spirit, had effectively
foretold a famine in Acts 11.28, issues a warning against
Paul's going to Jerusalem, which Paul again refuses to act
upon, convinced that it is the Lord's will for him to press on.
All this is significant. It suggests that an utterance made under
inspiration was not taken as infallible, but always needed testing. In 1 John 4.1 ff. there is an exhortation to test 'spirits',
that is, utterances claiming to be inspired; and the test is doctrinal. Whatever one may believe about the absolute and iner-
rant wisdom of God himself, it does not seem to be his way to
override the fallible, human persons who try to hear and
mediate his voice. Indeed, since the recipient is fallible and
human, his reception of the divine intimations is bound
always to be subject to error and to uncertainties of interpretation; and the same is true of his hearers. Notions of
absolute 'possession', in the sense that the deity speaks
through the prophet simply as a mouthpiece, overriding the

prophet's own personality, are not characteristic of biblical thought, even though many interpreters of the Bible have thought like this. Philo explicitly puts forward such a theory of inspiration, and there are Christians, from very early times onwards, who have held such notions;[21] but the Scriptures give them scant support.

As in the New Testament, so in the so-called Apostolic Fathers, there are instances of deep reverence for prophets, combined, however, with a shrewd discrimination. Thus, in the so-called Teaching of the Twelve Apostles (the *Didache*), there is a stern prohibition against 'testing' any prophet who speaks 'in Spirit', and yet, in the very next sentence, it is admitted that not everyone speaking 'in Spirit' is a prophet, but that he must 'have the ways of the Lord' (that is, follow Christlike principles), and that it is by their ways that false and true prophets are to be distinguished (cf. Matt. 7.15 ff.). And there follows (with certain obscurities which need not delay us here) the practical injunction not to believe a so-called prophet who uses his allegedly inspired authority to persuade people to give him food or money (*Did.* 11). So again, in *Did.* 13, it is assumed that true prophets can be distinguished from false, and that only the former are to be supported.[22]

The logic of all this is that inspired guidance never relieves the individual of his responsibility or allows decisions to be reached mechanically or infallibly. In the individual's decisions, conscience is an important factor. Although it is not a kind of god within nor an autonomous director, and although it has strict limitations (1 Cor. 4.3 f., '. . . I have nothing on my conscience; but that does not mean I stand acquitted. My judge is the Lord'), it is, so to speak, an organ of the personality which registers discomfort when its owner commits, or contemplates committing, what he believes to be an offence. Therefore, if it is to register Christian reactions, it needs to be trained within the Christian community.[23] So trained, it becomes an important factor for an individual when, in the light of inspired utterance and expert advice, he reaches a decision.

But the insights brought by the Spirit through Jesus Christ in his Church do not consist only of specific guidance. Still less

do they comprise secret, esoteric doctrines such as were che-
rished by gnostic sects in the ancient world. They are insights
into the character and nature of God and into his designs for
salvation. In Eph. 1.17 'a Spirit of wisdom' leads the recipient
to Christian understanding. In 5.18 f. the Spirit inspires the
music with which to praise God. The Spirit can give the vision
and the vigour that lead to the spontaneous creation of songs
of praise, as has been rediscovered in our own day in 'charismatic' groups all over the world. In Phil. 3.15 it is by 'revelation' that—so Paul assumes—further guidance will be given
to his friends in their understanding of God's will and character.

All in all, it is clear that Christians of the New Testament
looked to God for guidance. But they did not expect it to be infallible. It comes through inspired utterance, through mutual
consultation, through searching the conscience. And so it is
today. Christian decisions have to be reached by pooling all
the available expert information about the matter in hand
(whether the experts are Christians or not); by bringing to bear
such insights as Christians are given into the true function and
destiny of man in God's design; and by bringing all this in
prayer to God. The special 'ministry of the Word and the
Sacraments', to which clergy are ordained, is directly concerned with interpreting God's will and leading the worship in
which strength and courage may be found to implement it.

What happens if persons who claim to be inspired commit
their messages to writing? Is the result 'inspired writing',
'inspired scripture'? This is often alleged. But when one asks
precisely what it might mean for paper and ink to be 'inspired',
it becomes evident that this is a false notion—and certainly (if
one may indulge in a patent 'circle' of reasoning!) a doubtfully
scriptural one. As we have been reminded in discussing *epiclesis*, not much countenance is given, in Scripture or in theistic thought generally, to the notion that inanimate objects may
become penetrated by divine Spirit. God's Spirit acts in and
upon persons rather than upon things. A prophet may be
inspired, but can his writing be strictly so described? Was it
slices of inspiration that King Jehoiakim contemptuously
slashed off Jeremiah's scroll with his penknife and threw into

his brazier (Jer. 36.23)? There is a celebrated passage in 2 Tim. 3.16, declaring that all scripture is *theopneustos* (literally 'God-breathed'), and this is often translated 'inspired'. But it is an almost unique statement in the Bible; and, even here, it may be that 'uttered by God' is a better translation of the word.[24] This would mean that the words in Scripture were divinely '*ex*spired', 'breathed out'; it would make the words God's words rather than suggesting that the Scripture itself was penetrated by Spirit. It is true, of course, that several times in the New Testament the words of Scripture are recognized as the words of God. So Mark 12.36, Acts 1.16, 4.25, 28.25, and often in the Epistle to the Hebrews (9.8, 10.15, etc.). But, if so, one still needs to ask what this means and how it happens and in what sense, if any, this may be said of canonical Scripture and not of other writings.

Furthermore, even if a writer may have been divinely inspired, and is therefore in some sense authoritative, by what processes is the understanding of the writer's intention by the readers or hearers safeguarded? For a doctrine of the 'inspiredness' of a speaker to be significant, a doctrine of the inspiration of the *hearer* is required. Otherwise, how is one to know whether the hearer's or the reader's 'receiving apparatus' is getting the authoritative message? The chain of divine communication breaks if the last link is not inspired. This is the problem that 2 Pet. 1.20 seems to be wrestling with, when it says '. . . no one can interpret any prophecy of Scripture by himself'. The implication is that some authoritative interpretation is needed—not that of a private individual. And this is what the exegetical principles followed by most expositors (though with shining exceptions) right up to the beginning of the era of critical biblical scholarship were designed to provide: if you cannot make sense of the literal meaning, try allegory; but let all be in conformity with the creeds![25]

But what does inspiration mean anyway, at any stage?[26] It is constantly assumed that it means a divine guarantee of freedom from error. But ought it to be given this meaning? In general, God's way with men is to lift them up to be more fully human, not to override them and overpower them and use them as mere instruments—as though the Holy Spirit played

them as a flautist plays his flute. Precisely this analogy is
indeed used by the early Christian apologist Athenagoras;[27]
but what evidence is there that this is God's way? Besides, if
inspiration has any meaning, it would certainly be difficult to
confine it to the writers of what ultimately (under inspired
guidance?) became canonical Scripture. Few would wish to
deny that God's Spirit has been at work in all great creative art
and utterance everywhere, in literature, in music, in the visual
arts, and wherever there is authentic, creative imagination.
And although it has been observed in an earlier chapter that
biblical language tends not to use the word 'Spirit' in these
more general contexts, the point is that, call it what you will,
we instinctively recognize divine promptings in these activities,
and that, therefore, it would be illogical to refuse to recognize
authority of this sort outside Scripture. Thus, if the inspiration
of canonical Scripture means anything, it needs to be defined
as a special divine act of preservation from error, which is a
quite arbitrary definition, actually reducing the scope of God's
work to mere correctness of statement. And it would still tell us
nothing about how the allegedly infallible communication
could be infallibly received.

No. The distinctiveness of the canonical Scriptures of the
Old and New Testaments (so called by Christians) is that the
common mind of main-stream Christianity ultimately gave its
sanction to these writings, not as the only true ones, but as
those alone which the Church regarded as normative. And,
broadly speaking, the New Testament canon does in fact comprise precisely the earliest and the most authentic and representative documents of the Church's infancy—historically the
best evidence for Christian beginnings. There is no other body
of writings that fits that role; and although it is theoretically
possible that this is so merely because rival documents of equal
weight and antiquity were suppressed and no longer survive,
there is no evidence pointing in that direction. This does not
mean that the canonical Scriptures are without error, or that
they must not be critically sifted like any other documents of
antiquity. But it does mean that they serve a unique purpose
and are indispensable for that purpose, and therefore incomparably precious. And the ultimate selection of them was not a

sudden thing but a slow process of trial and error—the work, if you like, of the Holy Spirit in the understanding of Church leaders.

In sum, inspiration, while describing a profoundly important aspect of the Spirit's activities, is not a term that can be successfully used in the interests of the infallibility of canonical pronouncements or the uniqueness of Scripture (which lies not in its degree of inspiredness but in its character as chosen by the sifting processes of the Church's life to witness to the beginnings of Christianity). Neither does inspiration serve adequately—or so it has been argued here—to describe what main-stream Christianity sees as the uniqueness of Christ.

What it does serve to describe is the divine equipping of a person for a special task. In modern usage, we tend to break out from what has been noted as the biblical tendency to limit the concept of Spirit to God's activities within his 'chosen People'. We say 'that was an inspired interpretation' when a great conductor—probably not a conscious 'believer' at all—has made a new and living thing of a familiar symphony. But the point is a thoroughly biblical one, namely, the Spirit's work in equipping and empowering a person for a particular ministry: each need is met by the Spirit's endowment to match it.

And behind the particular ministries and the special needs lies the general equipping with Christian character, which is for all who will receive it—the foundation, as it were, on which the special gifts may be erected. Because God is the God who became incarnate in Jesus, the Spirit of God comes with the power to create something after the pattern of Christ's life in each believer. The Spirit is 'the Spirit of adoption', that is, the bringer of sonship. And as we are all alike enabled to cry 'Abba! Your will be done!', we are individually endowed also with the special gifts demanded by each task to which that cry directs us. There will be more to say about this when we come to the charismatic question.

VI. Spirit, Church, and Liturgy

IT would be simple and tidy to say that, as breath is to a body,
so is the Spirit of God to Christ's Body, the Church. St Augustine said, 'What the soul is for the body of a man, that is the
Holy Spirit for the body of Christ . . .; what the soul works in
all the members of the one body, that the Spirit works in the
whole of the Church.'[1] Karl Barth calls the Spirit the lifegiving
power or the awakening power by which Jesus the Lord builds
up Christians as his body in the world.[2] But the relation of the
Spirit to the Christian community, at least as it is reflected in
New Testament experience, cannot be defined quite so simply.
In the first place, the metaphor of the body is used by Paul in a
more limited way than is sometimes imagined. One is sometimes given to understand that the Pauline epistles are full of
the doctrine of the Church as the Body of Christ. But actually,
in Romans and I Corinthians, the use of this figure is limited.[3]
Primarily, its function is simply to describe the ideal relation of
one Christian to another, rather than the relation of Christians
to Christ. In other words, the metaphor operates 'laterally'
rather than 'vertically'. Thus, in Rom. 12.4 f., Paul says:

> '. . . just as in one body we have many limbs, and all the
> limbs have not the same function, so we, many as we are,
> are one body in Christ, and individually limbs of one
> another.'

Here, the phrase is not 'the body of Christ', but 'one body *in
Christ*'. The analogy of a number of different limbs and organs
harmoniously cooperating as an organic whole is applied
simply to a local congregation of Christians. The sense is similar, it may be said in parenthesis, in Gal. 3.28, although 'body'
is not used: 'You are all one person in Christ Jesus'. (Here 'one

70

person' rightly renders what in the Greek is simply 'one' in the masculine gender; had it been in the neuter, it might have meant not 'one person' but 'a unity'.) Of course it is highly significant, returning to Rom. 12.4 f., that all the Christians, who together constitute the body, are also described as 'in Christ'— that is, incorporated in him. But the body analogy as such is confined here to the 'lateral' relations of Christian to Christian. So in 1 Cor. 10.17, the words should probably be taken to mean that because, in the Eucharist, the congregation all share a single loaf (and thereby are confirmed in their participation in the one Christ), therefore they constitute a single 'body' or corporation:

> 'Because there is one loaf, we, many as we are, are one body; for it is one loaf of which we all partake.'

(Alternatively, the sense could be, 'we, many as we are, are one loaf, one body'—two metaphors, loaf and body, in quick succession, simply emphasising the unity, without attempting to explain it.) In the next chapter, 1 Cor. 11, Paul speaks of those who participate in the Lord's supper selfishly and greedily as 'failing to discern the body' (verse 29), and this may be a sort of *double entendre* referring both to the physical body of Christ as surrendered to death for us and to the 'body' of Christians, the congregation, to which the selfish participants are offering an insult.[4] Certainly, it is not enough foundation for a full doctrine of 'the Church as the body of Christ': 'the Church as a body', yes; but hardly as 'the body of Christ'. In 1 Cor. 12, however, at last one comes near to assured evidence for this idea. Verse 12 reads:

> 'For Christ is like a single body with its many limbs and organs, which, many as they are, together make up one body.'

Here, Christ himself is the body, and Christians (evidently) are its constituent parts. And the next verse is probably to be interpreted in the same direction:

> 'For indeed we were all brought into one body by baptism, in the one Spirit, whether we are Jews or Greeks,

whether slaves or free men, and that one Holy Spirit was
poured out for all of us to drink.'

It is uncertain whether the last words refer to giving drink to
the thirsty (as in the NEB version just quoted) or to watering
plants. But it is the first half of the verse that concerns the body
analogy; and here, although 'into one body' could, in the original Greek, mean 'so as to become one body' (the words are
simply 'we were all baptised into one body': 'brought' is merely
part of the English rendering), more probably the meaning is
that it was into one already existing body, namely the body of
Christ, that the converts were brought in baptism. If so, here,
as in verse 12, the body is Christ's own body, in a collective or a
corporate sense. However, by the time we reach verse 27, it
may be that, once again, the body denotes the organic unity of
Christians among themselves rather than Christ's own body.
The phrase 'Now you are Christ's body' need only mean 'you
are *a* body belonging to Christ'. As for 1 Cor. 6.15, 'Your
bodies are limbs of Christ', this, taken strictly at its face-value
and out of context, would imply that Christ was himself the
body and Christians his limbs. But, in the context, it looks as
though it must not be pressed; for these same limbs of Christ
may, by fornication, become 'limbs of a harlot'—which, if the
analogy were pressed, would yield the ridiculous sense that the
harlot was a 'corporate personality' with persons for limbs.

We are left, now, with the so-called Captivity Epistles—
those to the Ephesians and to the Colossians. Here, the Church
is spoken of more than once as Christ's body in contexts which
make it probable, though not in every case certain, that the
world-wide Church is meant, and not merely a local congregation, and that it is seen not merely as *a* corporation *belonging
to* Christ, but *the* body *of* Christ—Christ's own body. It is
notoriously true that in these epistles Christ is spoken of as the
head of the body, as though he were not, after all, viewed as
himself the entire body; and it has been argued that 'head' here
is not intended to be part of the body figure, but is used independently of it, to mean the origin or the ruler (a sense which it
can carry in Semitic thought). But whether this is so or not, certainly the Church is very closely related to Christ, and it may

be that here, at last, there is a firm use of the figure for the Church as, indeed, Christ's very Body. The relevant passages are Col. 1.18, 24; 2.19; 3.15; Eph. 1.23; 2.15 f.; 4.4, 12–16. Not so relevant, or, in some instances, not relevant at all, are Col. 1.22; 2.11, 17; Eph. 5.23, 30.

Thus, to sum up: in the Pauline epistles, the function of the body analogy is primarily to describe the 'lateral' relation of Christian to Christian, rather than the 'vertical' relation of Christian to Christ. That the Church is Christ's body usually means, in the Pauline epistles (though with a few exceptions), that it is an organized community *belonging* to Christ; and Christians are more often seen as limbs and organs of the Christian community than as directly limbs and organs of Christ himself. This is true, despite the fact that nowhere in the New Testament is the Christian community called the body of *Christians.*[5] Certainly, it is called the body (or, more correctly, *a* body) of Christ; but this seems to mean mainly an organised whole *belonging to* him, rather than his own body. The main exceptions are, first, 1 Cor. 12.12 f. Here, the body does indeed seem to be identified with Christ, as the organism which is actually Christ himself. Then, secondly, perhaps this sense is the most natural one also in certain passages in the Captivity Epistles (Eph. 1.23, 4.12; Col. 1.18, 24).

However, even if the maximum allowance is made for the need to modify some of the current conceptions of Pauline 'body'-doctrine, it still remains a most impressive fact that it is only by virtue of its being 'in Christ' that the Church becomes an organic, interrelated whole. 'In Christ', 'in the Lord', and similar expressions are used by Paul in many different ways; but among these are a few which seem to reflect a remarkable sense that the risen Christ, the Lord, is more than a divine 'individual'.[6] He is an inclusive Person, in whom Christians and communities of Christians live and move and have their being. Christ the Lord is the environment of Christian life—the very 'place' of Christian existence. Broadly, then, Paul's habit is to think of Christians, singly and collectively, as 'in Christ' or 'in the Lord'.

Conversely, he tends to think of the Holy Spirit as in each Christian. Karl Barth describes 'in Spirit' as the subjective counterpart of the objective 'in Christ'.[7] Rarely, Paul does refer to Christ as 'indwelling' each individual (Rom. 8.10, Gal. 2.20), or as among Christians and 'indwelling' the Christian community (Col. 1.27?). But this is only rarely. And although 'in Spirit' occurs fairly often, it seldom, if ever, seems to mean anything comparable to the incorporative phrase 'in Christ' or 'in the Lord' (which is perhaps what Barth's remark is getting at). Roughly speaking, the tendency is to speak of Christians as 'dwelling' in Christ, whereas the Spirit is spoken of as 'dwelling' in Christians. The presence of the Spirit is a *sine qua non* of being a Christian (Rom. 8.9, '. . . if a man does not possess the Spirit of Christ, he is no Christian'). Christians know themselves to be Christians precisely because they know themselves possessed of the Spirit.

This, as is sometimes pointed out,[8] is the very reverse of what one will be told in some Christian traditions today. One will be told 'You must believe that you have the Spirit because you are a baptised and confirmed Christian. It may be that you will not be given any visible sign of it. Your confirmation may seem to make no difference. But believe it, because this is what being a Christian means'. But the New Testament, by contrast, seems to say, 'If you want to be assured that you are really a member of the Church, really incorporated in Christ, look at the manifest presence of the Spirit.' Examples of this are the following:

Rom. 8.16:

> 'In that cry ["Abba! Father!"] the Spirit of God joins with our spirit in testifying that we are God's children.'

Gal. 4.6:

> 'To prove that you are sons, God has sent into our hearts the Spirit of his Son, crying "Abba! Father!"'

(Here, admittedly, the NEB's 'To prove that' renders a single Greek particle, *hoti*, which can mean 'because' as well as 'that', and could, therefore, be here rendered 'because'; but, in the context, the former seems the more likely.)

1 John 3.24:

> '. . . And this is how we can make sure that he dwells within us: we know it from the Spirit he has given us.'

1 John 4.13:

> 'Here is the proof that we dwell in him and he dwells in us: he has imparted his Spirit to us.'

With this may be compared John 13.35, where the presence of love is the evidence appealed to:

> 'If there is this love among you, then all will know that you are my disciples.'

Thus, the question arises whether the Spirit ought to be signalised by perceptible symptoms. The next chapter will attempt to discuss this.

Meanwhile, it is clear at least that the Spirit is 'in' Christians as such, and 'in' the Church. The Spirit is the mode of Christ's presence with his people. As G. S. Hendry says: 'In the experience of the Church the presence of the Holy Spirit was known, not as an alternative to, but as a mode of, the presence of the living Christ . . .'[9] If Christians are all together incorporated in Christ, it is by the Spirit that Christ comes within each of them. Curiously enough, however, the New Testament never, as we have seen, actually exploits the analogy of breath and body, as later writers do. It does not say, in so many words, that, as breath (spirit) is to a body, so is the Spirit (the breath of God) to the Church. Eph. 4.3 speaks of 'the unity of the Spirit', meaning, apparently, the organic harmony brought by the Spirit (cf. 1 Cor. 12.13 as quoted above); and, in verse 4, it comes near to relating the Spirit to the Church as breath to body, with the words 'there is one body and one Spirit'; but it stops short of explicitly drawing the analogy. Elsewhere, in Eph. 2.22, the Spirit is brought into relation with the building of which Christ is the cornerstone, in the vague phrase, 'in Spirit'; and in 1 Cor. 3.16, the Spirit of God dwells in the community which is called God's temple. But the phrase in 2 Cor. 13.13 commonly rendered 'the fellowship of the Holy Spirit'

probably does *not* mean the community created and vitalised
by the Holy Spirit. *Koinonia*, the word translated 'fellowship',
is constantly misconstrued in Christian devotional writing, as
though it were a concrete noun, 'the fellowship'. It is not. It is
an abstract noun meaning 'joint participation', 'sharing'.[10]
Certainly, that joint participation in the Holy Spirit does lead
to fellowship; but the fellowship is the result. The cause is the
joint sharing in the Spirit (cf. 1 Cor. 12.13, Eph. 4.4 referred to
earlier). It is true that experience sometimes works the other
way round. It is often through the already existing Church that
a person will be brought into participation in the Spirit: it has
been well pointed out[11] that Eph. 4.4–6 represents the order of
experience—through the Church to the Spirit, and so to the
Lord Christ and so to God the Father. But the point still holds
good: fellowship is the result, basically and originally, of
jointly sharing in the Spirit. Mostly, then, the Spirit is thought
of as participated in jointly by all, but bestowed on each individual severally. It is true that the authority and validity of the
whole organization is sometimes seen as under the control of
the Holy Spirit. Thus, John 20.22 f. associates acceptance into
or exclusion from the community with the gift of the Spirit to
the body of the apostles; the elders of Ephesus are spoken of in
Acts 20.28 as appointed by the Holy Spirit to be overseers; and
in Eph. 4.11, apostles, prophets, evangelists, and the rest constitute the gift of the ascended Christ, which elsewhere (e.g.
Acts 2.33) is identified with the Spirit.[12] But mainly, the Holy
Spirit is within each person.

The presence of the Spirit marks the community as true
Israel,[13] and is the guarantee that God will ultimately claim
and redeem his people. It is a sign of the beginning of the fulfilment of God's final purpose. So the Holy Spirit is the first
fruits, guaranteeing the holiness of the whole crop, the 'earn-
est' or 'deposit', guaranteeing the full payment, or the seal,
marking God's ownership and (if the metaphor be pressed)
perhaps guaranteeing that the property will reach its proper
destination (Rom. 8.23, 2 Cor. 1.22, 5.5, Eph. 1.14). Thus, the
Spirit's presence is associated with entering the Church which
is thus characterised. It is the hallmark of being a Christian;
and it is the Spirit of God's Son, which enables Christians

themselves to become Sons of God, addressing him, as Jesus did, with the intimate obedience of 'Abba! dear Father! your will be done!' (Mark 14.36, Rom. 8.15, Gal. 4.6). The Spirit creates in Christians the character of Christ. It is by the Spirit that Christ comes into a life. It is true that the Spirit may be resisted: it is a free choice; and the matter of sinning against the Spirit has already been discussed. But to as many as respond to the Spirit (if John 1.12 may be thus adapted), he gives the right to become sons, children, of God.

This brings us to two vital questions—the relation of the Holy Spirit to sacraments and to prayer. The question of the relation of the Holy Spirit to baptism is notoriously problematic.[14] It will return in the next chapter, in the consideration of charismatic experiences. For the present, it can at least be said that, whatever the relation between the two, both water baptism and the coming of the Spirit are seen in the Acts as regular and normal factors in becoming a Christian—whether the coming of the Spirit is before, at, or after the water-ritual. But this is not so easily established for other writers. In John 3.5, the meaning of begetting 'by water and Spirit' is much debated. Instinctively, a churchman hears in it a reference to water-baptism accompanied by the presence of the Spirit. The late Rudolf Bultmann, however, in a famous commentary,[15] argued that 'water and' was an interpolation, alien to the original writer's intention. He based his view on the absence of any mention of water in verse 6, and on his theory, based on other features of the Gospel, of a sacramentalist interpolator. J. D. G. Dunn inclines to the view that 'water and Spirit' form a single phrase which uses 'water' as a symbol of the life-giving power of the Spirit.[16] H. Odeberg, perhaps more ingeniously than plausibly, wanted to see in the water an allusion to semen: the begetting of a Christian is by *spiritual*, not *material*, semen (just as John 1.13 alludes to divine birth, in contrast to the physical processes).[17] In the Pauline epistles, it is impossible to find demonstrative proof that Spirit and the water of baptism go together. In 1 Cor. 12.13, the water-metaphor would certainly be appropriate if literal water was in mind: '. . . we were all brought into one body by baptism, in the one Spirit, whether we are Jews or Greeks, whether slaves or free men, and that one Holy Spirit was poured out for all of us to drink'. Yet admittedly, the NEB by putting a comma between 'baptism' and 'in the one Spirit' is removing an ambiguity which the Greek retains, for it *could* be 'baptism in the one Spirit'—using 'baptism' not literally with reference to water but as a metaphor for 'deluging' with Spirit; and, in the second half of the verse, it is impossible to interpret the verb ('poured out for all of us to drink') otherwise than metaphorically, though it is possible that the metaphor is from irrigating plants rather than from providing the thirsty with a draught of water. Even in the Acts, Spirit-baptism seems to be *contrasted* with water-baptism at 1.5 and 11.16; and at 8.16 there is a notorious gap between the two. But it is in the Acts, nevertheless, that water-baptism is evidenced as usual, and Spirit is more than once expressly associated with it, even when the water ritual and the coming of the Spirit are not simultaneous: Acts 2.38, 8.16 f., 9.17–19, 10.44, 47; cf. 8.38 f., 16.33 f. The precise relation, however, of the coming of the Holy Spirit to the water and to the imposition of hands is notoriously problematical. In Acts 2.38 water seems to be a means towards the receiving of Spirit. In Acts 8.16 f., however, the Samaritan converts, though already baptised in water, receive no Spirit until apostolic hands have been laid upon them; and in Acts 1.5 and 11.16, as has just been noted, there is a contrast between water-baptism and Spirit-baptism, although this does not in itself imply that there is no connexion between the two or even that the two are not normally complementary.

The association of the Holy Spirit with the Lord's Supper or Holy Communion is not explicit in the New Testament, though it is utterly reasonable and right to pray God to send his Holy Spirit upon the worshippers (even if not upon the ele-ments—see pp. 53f. above). Besides if the Christian sacraments act as a 'focus' for the meeting of God's generosity and man's response, can one exclude the coming of the Spirit at that focal point? The German language provides a useful assonance—'Gabe und Aufgabe', 'gift and task'; and this well sums up the meeting of God's generosity and the believer's response to the challenge inherent in it. It is the meeting of these two that a sacrament focuses and clinches, and, in clinching, positively effects or furthers. Therefore, the Spirit of God, as the gift that makes the task possible, inspiring our obedient 'Abba! your will be done!', must necessarily accompany a sacrament. There may be a hint of the association of the Holy Spirit and the Eucharist at Heb. 10.29, where 'the blood of the covenant' and 'the Spirit of grace' are found together.

The awareness of the Spirit's presence may not coincide with the sacrament. It may come at some other time. There may be different levels in a single experience—the mystical, the sacramental, the emotional and the psychological; and there is no reason why these should necessarily coincide in time: the different levels and 'foci' of the one relationship may well be, so to speak, 'staggered'. Emotionally, one may well be more aware at some other time than at the time of a sacrament. But all the different facets belong to a single jewel. The giving and receiving of a ring and the pledging of troth either to other is not (one hopes) either the beginning or the end of the growth of love; but that does not mean that the sacramental moment is not both a 'focus' of the relationship, and an effective clinching of it.

It is possible that a reference to the Spirit in the sacraments is contained in 1 John 5. In the AV, verses 6 to 8 contain a threefold doctrinal statement about the Father, the Word, and the Holy Ghost; but it is universally recognized that this is a spurious interpolation from a late text (cf. note 8, Chap. 3). Without it, the passage reads:

> 'This is he who came with water and blood: Jesus Christ. He came, not by water alone, but by water and blood; and there is the Spirit to bear witness, because the Spirit is truth. For there are three witnesses, the Spirit, the water, and the blood, and these three are in agreement.'

It is impossible to be certain what is meant. But fairly clearly, a 'docetic' Christology is being refuted—that is, a conception of incarnation only in appearance ('docetic' means 'seeming') and a refusal to believe in a real union of the divine and human in Jesus. It is known that a theory was actually current that the divine descended on Jesus at his baptism, but left him again

before his suffering and death on the cross. It was imagined
that the divine could not suffer. It was deduced, therefore, that
the divine was not permanently united with the human to the
length of going through death. The divine merely came alongside temporarily, and departed before the end. Exactly this is
what Muslims read in the Qur'an.[18] But 1 John 5.6–8 hotly
opposes this. No, says the writer, Jesus Christ (the whole
Christ, divine and human) 'came', not only through the water
of his baptism but through the blood of the cross. The union
was complete and permanent: Jesus, our divine Saviour, suffered and died.

It is possible that there may also be some subtle connection,
impossible now to pin down, between the narrative in John
19.34 of the water and blood that flowed from the Lord's side,
and this passage in 1 John 5. But what concerns the present
inquiry is the place of the Spirit in this testimony—this bearing
witness by the Spirit. If 'blood' means real death, and if the
writer's point is that Jesus Christ really died as a whole person,
not as a human vehicle now destitute of the divine freight it
once carried, what is meant by the triad, 'Spirit, water, blood'?
Possibly, 'Spirit' here means the presence of the Holy Spirit
among Christians. They have received the Spirit through Jesus
Christ, and this confirms the validity of their faith in him as the
divine-human Saviour, both baptised and crucified. Perhaps
there is a further reference to sacraments—the water of baptism and the 'blood' of the Eucharist. In that case, does 'Spirit'
refer to the fact that the Spirit is recognized as present in the
sacraments? On the strength of this suggestion, some scholars
have gone on to ask where and when the ritual expressing the
coming of the Spirit preceded baptism in water. In some traditions, from early times, chrism, that is anointing with oil, has
been practised at baptism as a symbol of the endowment or
'christing' of each Christian with the Spirit's unction. Usually,
chrismation followed baptism. But there were some early
Syrian rites where chrismation came first; and an attempt has
been made to identify the provenance of 1 John by this supposed allusion to an unusual baptismal sequence.[19] Probably,
however, the words 'water and blood' so naturally cohered together in a single phrase that it was immaterial which side of

the 'bracket' (so to say) the word 'Spirit' was placed. In any case, this writer actually used the word 'chrism' in another passage (2.20 ff.) in a more general way—possibly, as C. H. Dodd urged,[20] to indicate the possession of spiritual truth rather than as a direct allusion to Spirit in baptism. However, it may well be right to class 1 John 5.6 ff. among references to the Holy Spirit's presence at the entry into and the maintenance of Christian membership in the sacraments.

The place of the Holy Spirit in worship generally is a question that still requires closer attention than it is usually accorded. Several observations may be made. First, it is noteworthy that the Holy Spirit is, in a sense, the subject rather than the object of prayer. 'The Spirit constantly leads our attention away from himself to Jesus Christ', writes Berkhof.[21] It is the Holy Spirit's voice within us that cries 'Abba!' (Rom. 8.15, Gal. 4.6). We do not address the Spirit in prayer; rather, the Holy Spirit within us enables us to address God. Similarly, Paul says that the Spirit intercedes for us, even when we are, of ourselves, unable to frame words (Rom. 8.26; cf. verse 34, where Christ is the intercessor). In Rev. 22.17, it is the Spirit and Christ's Bride, the Church, who together address Jesus Christ, saying 'Come!' In Eph. 6.17, 'the sword of the Spirit', in the Christian warrior's armour, is 'the Word of God' or 'the utterance of God', which seems to mean the words which the Spirit enables us to speak. The NEB renders: '. . . take that which the Spirit gives you—the words that come from God.' This is the sword by which Christians on trial can fight victoriously. It is a reminder of the temptation story in Matthew and Luke, which is associated with the Spirit's power and guidance—Matt. 4.1, Luke 4.1; cf. Mark 1.12—; and of the promise that words will be provided by the Spirit, in Mark 13.11, parallel to Matt. 10.20; cf. Luke 21.15. So, once again, the Spirit utters the words that Christians have to say: the Spirit enables their utterance to be in line with God's design.

Thus, the Holy Spirit is most characteristically experienced as God immanent in man; and it is in keeping with this that the Spirit's voice turns out to be, as it were, the voice of God addressing himself from within man. It is like a deeply sympathetic parent or friend not imposing on the other, but somehow

evoking from the other a kind of echo of himself: '. . . God
himself at work in us, witnessing, responding, interceding', as
the late C. C. Richardson said.[22] Accordingly, prayers
addressed to the Holy Spirit are rare. Non-existent in the New
Testament, they are infrequent in later liturgy. The best known
exceptions are the invocation in the Litany ('O God the Holy
Ghost, proceding from the Father and the Son: have mercy
upon us miserable sinners'), and the ancient hymns, *Veni Creator Spiritus*, and *Veni sancte Spiritus*, each with many different translations and imitations. Even the Whitsunday collect is
not addressed to the Spirit but to God, with a petition to him to
send the Spirit; and, according to Anglican rites at least, at a
confirmation, the Bishop does not invoke the Spirit but prays
God to enable the confirmand to increase in the Holy Spirit. It
is a question whether the invocation of the Spirit is desirable or
not. At the end of this book, there is raw material for prayer for
or about the Spirit within the biblical categories, and without
such invocation.

Secondly, there is in the Church's hymnody (or at least has
been, until recently) a marked shortage of hymns about the
Holy Spirit in any corporate aspect. There are descriptions,
simply, of what happened, publicly and collectively, at Pentecost; but otherwise there is a marked individualism and 'private' character about these hymns. Harriet Auber's 'Our blest
Redeemer', says (in rather unctuous language) much that is
true about the work of the Spirit in the individual Christian,
but nothing directly about Christian unity or corporate life.
Even Edwin Hatch's 'Breathe on me, Breath of God', which is
a strong, unemotional, deeply Pauline hymn, is concerned
only with the individual's experience.

This tendency at first seems a serious defect.[23] Is not the
Holy Spirit conspicuously the Spirit bringing unity (Eph. 4.3)?
Is it not distorting the proportions of Christian fellowship to
concentrate on the individual's experience? Yet, on reflexion,
it may be true to Christian experience to associate the Spirit
especially with individual life. It has already been noted that
the New Testament reflects an understanding of the Holy
Spirit as essentially a mediator, in each individual, of the character of Christ, whereas the corporate life of the Christian

congregation as an organic body is seen as maintained, rather, by incorporation in Christ—though certainly this involves also joint participation in the Spirit. Perhaps we must recognize, then, that the way in which the Spirit of God and of Christ brings unity is by breaking down in each individual the pride, the unforgivingness, and the suspicions that keep persons apart from one another; and that hymns, in their preoccupation with the Spirit in the individual, may, after all, be in the main faithful to the instincts of the New Testament. Perhaps we must admit that the wind or breath of God that, in Ezek. 37, gives life to the dry bones of a whole army, symbolising the entire nation, has its counterpart in characteristically Christian experience only insofar as the Spirit, jointly participated in by all, enters each individual and brings 'bone to bone'—conferring such life and sensitivity as, in the end, does make for corporate aliveness. Perhaps it is precisely this concern for each individual that is part of the distinctive emphasis of the Christian gospel, implemented by the Spirit.

But if so, it is vital to add that it is equally characteristic of the gospel not to leave it there. The essentially corporate dimension of Christian life is inescapably clear. An individual cannot in fact receive the Spirit and find life at all without getting his relations with others right and becoming a part of the 'body'. Nobody can grow to the full stature of personhood in isolation, for personhood is essentially in relationship (cf. Eph. 4.13, 'So shall we all at last attain to the unity inherent in our faith . . .'). Thus, we are back again at the mysterious and difficult borderland where we ask whether the Spirit does not, somehow, actually constitute relationship. It is the question we encountered in discussing trinity. It was then observed, however, that it is difficult to attribute personality to a relationship. The one thing that is clear is that the receiving of the Holy Spirit by each individual is basic to Christian life; and that this, in turn, is unthinkable without the individual's being in a right relation with fellow Christians. If this is what Christian liturgy and hymns are saying, perhaps they are on the right lines.

VII. The Charismatic Question

ONE of the most remarkable and hopeful features in the Christian scene today is what goes under the broad description of the charismatic movement. If one leaves aside details of precise definition (as between 'charismatic', 'Pentecostal', and other terms), and does not attempt to tell again the history of this very variegated phenomenon (for it has been ably done by others),[1] the fact, in outline, is that, for many years, in practically every part of the world, and across all distinctions of tradition and denomination, a great upsurge of the power of God has been experienced. It has been experienced both in the unstructured, sectarian type of congregation, and in the traditional and highly structured Churches, including the Roman Catholic Church itself. It has been evidenced by a rebirth of sheer love and mutual concern, and by moral renewal, as well as by manifestations such as speaking with tongues and the power to mediate God's healing to those who are ill.

Inevitably, it is these latter manifestations that have attracted most attention and also caused most dissension. In addition to their being exciting and spectacular, and therefore easily overrated, one of the dangers attending visible and audible manifestations is that, precisely because they may be observed and one can therefore tell objectively whether or not they are present, they bring with them a gratifying assurance which is not available in the same way in the case of invisible attitudes and motives. Consequently, they too easily come to be regarded as the sole or main criterion of genuine Christian experience, and those who have not exhibited them come to be rated as inferior, second-class Christians. There is no need for this to happen, but happen it sometimes does, with devastating results.

Sometimes, those who have experienced an access of new, spiritual symptoms subsequently to their original admission to the Christian Church have claimed that this 'baptism in Spirit', as a distinctively 'second blessing', is a *sine qua non* of true Christian life, and that it is attested as such by the New Testament. They appeal to passages such as Acts 8.15 f. and 19.5 f. In Acts 8.15 f., the Samaritans, though already baptised by Philip, do not receive the Spirit until Peter and John come and lay their hands on them. In Acts 19.5 f., a group of persons already baptised with John the Baptist's baptism receive the Spirit only when Paul causes them to be baptised into the name of the Lord Jesus and lays hands on them, whereupon they begin to speak with tongues and prophesy. In these passages baptism in water seems to be distinguished, as inadequate or incomplete, from the authentic reception of the Spirit. In the face of this, it is disappointing that the New Testament's evidence for the relation between baptism in water and the Holy Spirit's coming, discussed in the preceding chapter, is so obscure. On the whole, however, the most competent works of scholarship on this question[2] hold that the 'pentecostal' interpretation tends to strain the texts illegitimately, and that it is wrong to interpret the evidence to mean that a 'two-stage' process is the norm or is a pointer to a theological principle.

In any case, the really important question is whether the Holy Spirit has been received, not whether this was simultaneously with baptism or not. In the New Testament, 'the Twelve' themselves—the most intimate associates of Jesus—are not stated ever to have received water-baptism in the name of Jesus Christ, though some of them may have been baptised, like Jesus himself, by John the Baptist. But, in the Acts tradition, they received the Holy Spirit in the new and distinctively Christian way from the ascended Christ at Pentecost (Acts 2.33). It is a question whether the account in John 20.22 of how the risen Christ bestowed Holy Spirit on the disciples on Easter Day is to be regarded as the Johannine parallel to Pentecost, or interpreted in some more harmonising way.[3] (Incidentally, when did the Fourth Evangelist think that Thomas received the Spirit? He was not with the others when Jesus 'breathed on them'—John 20, 22, 24.) At any rate, if the Spirit

is truly present—whenever this happens, and whatever its relation to water-baptism—then, whether there are immediately
visible signs or not, there will certainly be the beginnings of the
basic, less demonstrative, but all-important qualities that
mark the Christian character. The word 'charismatic' is often
applied expressly to groups which have the visible, audible
symptoms; but this is exactly what St Paul refused to do. In
dealing with the Christians at Corinth, some of whom were
excited and elated by their 'spiritual' accomplishments, St Paul
showed a masterly tact and firmness of grasp. They called
these gifts *pneumatika*, spiritual things; he did not reject the
word, but insisted whenever possible, on calling them *charismata*, which means simply 'gifts'.⁴ They singled out the more
spectacular; and Paul himself is careful not to disparage these.
Possibly the words 'do not stifle inspiration' in 1 Thess. 5.19
(literally, 'do not quench the Spirit') may be an injunction to
give full scope to them. Certainly in 1 Cor. 14.18 he claims that
he has them himself in a high degree. But he insists on lumping
all the *charismata* together, so that the signs of the Spirit—the
gifts, that is, generously bestowed by God for no merit of our
own, and 'empowered', as it were, by the Spirit—include
moral qualities every bit as much as the more spectacular abili-
ties. Indeed, if the more spectacular gifts are being used in a
rivalrous and boastful way, it shows that the Christians at
Corinth are at a pitifully elementary stage, and are far from
'spiritual' (1 Cor. 3.3 ff.). And Paul deliberately puts his exquisite lyric of love (1 Cor. 13) in the middle of his argument
about spiritual gifts; it is not a bit of decoration, but the very
hinge of his argument. The gifts, without love, are worthless.

In Gal. 5.22, the 'crop' yielded by the Spirit is described
wholly in terms of personal relations and qualities of character: love, joy, peace; patience, kindness, goodness; fidelity,
gentleness, self-control. And the opposite—the results of the
'flesh' (that is, not necessarily gross sensuality but self-concern
which leaves God out of account)—are, more than half of
them, sins of rivalry and jealousy and hatred. 'The Baptism of
the Spirit', writes Professor A. D. Galloway, 'thought be-
tokened for Pentecostals by the exterior sign of speaking with
tongues, is in its substance a deep, inner, peaceful communion

with God in the Spirit'. And he goes on to quote from another writer who speaks of a believer's being immersed in the power of the Spirit.[5]

All this is not to belittle 'tongues' or healing, and Paul certainly does not do so. The gift of tongues, as it is known today, seems usually to be a spontaneous welling up of a special language. It is not recognisable as any known language, but it expresses joy or exultation or eager hope. Paul points out, in 1 Cor. 14, that this is, in itself, of little or no value to a congregation, for they cannot understand it. It is private to the individual, and is of value only to him or her. But, for him or her, it is, it would seem, a significant outlet of pent-up praise or emotion too deep, too intense, for words: it is a precious mode of private devotion. It relaxes and releases the soul for adoration. Just as a person may get up and dance for joy or make gestures of adoration because he cannot contain himself, so at another moment the exultation and adoration may spill over into these otherwise unknown words. Paul says that if tongues are to be of value in the congregation, there must be an interpreter there (1 Cor. 14.28). But it must be confessed that, at any rate today, what is offered as interpretation (generally by someone other than the one speaking in tongues) is often very general; and, although it may have independent value, it can hardly be more successful as an interpretation of the tongues themselves than the notoriously hopeless attempt to describe the 'meaning' of music or ballet, of a poem, or of abstract art. Inevitably, a prose interpretation, even at its best, cannot convey what the original inspired, artistic creation means. That was precisely the point of not using prose in the first place.

Sometimes, but more rarely, it appears that the ability to speak a known human language is bestowed on one who does not himself already know it. It seems that certain instances of this in our own day are well attested. This appears to be what is intended in the account of the day of Pentecost in Acts 2— unless an even more surprising phenomenon is meant, namely, that, whatever the apostles themselves said, it reached each hearer in his own language (rather like a miraculous multilingual translation service!). However, this part of the Pentecost story may be intended simply as a symbolical way of

saying that Pentecost reversed the curse of Babel (Gen. 11).
The alienated and scattered nations are reconciled in the language of the Spirit. One is reminded of the hexameter printed
in the Bagster Bibles:[6]

> '*multae terricolis linguae, coelestibus una*
> (men on earth have many tongues:
> those in heaven but one).'

In this sense, the story is full of significance. But it is difficult to
understand what serious value such a gift, literally interpreted,
may have today.

'If the Pentecostal Church had spread love as they have
spread speaking in tongues', wrote Juan Carlos Ortiz, 'the
world would have written another history of this century'.[7]
But, in fairness, charismatics often urge that 'tongues' are not
particularly important; and, in some cases, they dissociate
themselves from the Pentecostals, strictly so called. Obviously,
motive and attitude are all-important, as Paul saw.

As for the gifts of healing, there is little doubt that Jesus himself, and, in a measure, his disciples, healed illnesses by touch
and by word, without medicaments or surgery; and this
phenomenon is by no means confined to Christianity or to any
one religion or period. It happens today in a great variety of
places and circumstances. How far such healings go it is difficult to find really sound evidence for determining. Certainly
there is ample evidence for the cure of what may be called psychosomatic disorders in this way. But is there adequately
tested evidence for the healing, by word or touch, of so-called
'organic' disease? Can fractures be thus healed? Can an amputated limb be restored? Can the dead be raised? (And, anyway,
how define death?) Sweeping claims are made about all these
achievements, but it is a question how good the evidence is.

But, once again, as with 'tongues', the motive is all-important. This is movingly illustrated by an anecdote told by
Archbishop Anthony Bloom and quoted by Bishop J. V.
Taylor.[8] A person engaged in intense intercession becomes so
vividly aware of the divine presence that he loses sight of the
one for whom he is praying; but, as he is drawn deeper and
deeper into the divine presence, he rediscovers his friend *there*,

at the heart of the divine love. That is the proper perspective in prayer for healing. But if the healing ability is used for boasting or for material gain or for prestige then it is demonic. Indeed, if even health itself, desirable though it may seem, is the sole objective, rather than reconciliation with God and man, then there is something wrong. And if 'spiritual' healing is practised in defiance of medical aid or as an expression of contempt for it, or so as to exclude it, there must, surely, be something wrong. It must take its place in the overall perspective of God's total will for all concerned, and in the context of Christian ministry of all kinds, with grateful acknowledgement of professional skills, and of all constructive powers capable of being offered to God.

In any case, it would appear that a spiritual gift that needs to accompany the gift of healing is the ability to discern when it is God's will that there should be such healing. Only in such cases will the healer know with the necessary confidence that he may ask God for healing. This is suggested by Acts 14.9 where Paul 'sees' that the cripple has the faith to be cured. A story from Ceylon a few decades ago is relevant here.[9] The Singhalese artist Bezalel (so named, on his conversion, after the Mosaic artist-craftsman in Exod. 31.1 f.) was restored to health in grave illness when his fellow Christians had united in prayer for him. A friend went to visit him, and put a testing question. 'Bezalel', he said, 'prayer has restored you. So, if ever you fall ill again, I suppose you need only to ask for prayer, and you will be certain that you will recover?' 'Oh, no!', he said (and this was exactly what his friend had hoped for); 'oh, no! now I know that I am always in God's hands, whether for life or death.' No doubt Christians ought to have more faith. No doubt those who exercise and promote the ministry of healing through prayer are doing a fine service, and more Christians ought to share their faith and faithfulness. But it must not be an end in itself; nor can it be satisfactorily viewed outside the context of all Christian ministries, including the medical skills; nor, it seems, can it be effectively performed without some insight into God's will in each particular instance.

But, after all, why are phenomena such as 'tongues' and healing through prayer (and even so strange a phenomenon as levitation—Acts 8.39?) classed as distinctively manifestations of the Spirit? Why not simply of God's presence? Or why not of the presence of the risen Lord Jesus Christ? Is there something in them that is peculiarly associated with the Spirit's work? The answer is, perhaps, mainly in the fact that 'tongues' and other gifts for the Church's welfare are expressly associated with the Spirit in the Acts and the Pauline epistles. But it is also in keeping with a general tendency in the New Testament, which has been already remarked on. Whereas Christians and Christian congregations tend to be thought of as incorporated in Christ—living and acting in the environment which is Christ—it is by the Spirit, within each believer and permeating the congregation, that the characteristics of being in Christ are produced. 'Spirit' seems to be by far the most appropriate term for God's presence, through Jesus Christ, in the believer.

It is perhaps surprising that there is very little direct evidence that Jesus himself spoke with 'tongues'. Scholars have debated whether he did so, and have appealed to one passage or another (specially Luke 10.21, where Jesus' exultation is associated with the Spirit—different in Matt. 11.25).[10] But the evidence is not conclusive. That he healed, however, cannot be denied without doing violence to the best attested strands of tradition.

One thing is clear, and this is that nothing is gained by an attempt to 'work oneself up' into an ability to speak with tongues or to exhibit other spiritual gifts or qualities. Whatever comes, comes, if it is authentic, as a gift, and simply as the Christian obediently seeks God and seeks to do his will. And when a gift such as 'tongues' does come, those who are familiar with it assure us that it is never 'ecstatic', if that word is taken to mean out of the subject's control. It is not like the overriding, irresistible 'possession' of the Pythian priestess at the oracle of Delphi, or even the frenzy of some of the guilds of prophets in the Old Testament (see above pp. 60 f.). It is exercised consciously and controlledly and in such a way that, if the gift is available, the use of it can be started and terminated at will.

'Charism' (from Greek *charizomai*, 'to bestow a gift') is a gift from God empowered by his Spirit. It may also be described metaphorically as an 'anointing' or 'chrism' (from

Greek *chriō*, 'to anoint'). As such, it is the ordinary, *sine qua non* of basic Christian existence. In 1 John 2.20 ff., the writer appeals to his readers as possessing an 'anointing', a 'chrism'. This appears to mean an endowment with God's Spirit as guide and instructor, to keep them in the ways of truth (see above, p. 81). It is assumed as something belonging to them simply as Christians. For Christians it is axiomatic, and its functions are comparable to those attributed in John 14, 15, and 16 to the Holy Spirit as Paraclete. Similarly, Paul can use the same metaphor of anointing or 'christing' to describe the Christian's endowment with Spirit (2 Cor. 1.21; cf. Acts 10.38, with reference to Christ himself). 'Christ' or 'Messiah' means one who has been anointed; and for Jesus Christ, and, in their measure, for Christians, the anointing is not with literal unguent but with the Holy Spirit. This endowment with Spirit is seen, as we have been reminded again and again, as indispensable for every Christian (cf. Rom. 8.9). It is of secondary importance what particular form the manifestations of the Spirit take. Over and above the indispensable 'crop' of the Spirit in terms of basic, Christian qualities of character (Gal. 5.22), the additional gifts may vary according to circumstances and needs.

This is, perhaps, the explanation of what at first seems perplexing: the fact that some who already have the Spirit are said to be endowed with the Spirit again. There are several references in the Acts to such further endowments, which evidently constitute equipment for special purposes. There is a sense in which the disciples of Jesus, like any other devout Jews (or, for that matter, devoutly religious persons of whatever faith), must have received the Spirit even before the death of Christ. After the death and resurrection, however, they have a new and distinctive experience, such as is reflected in John 20.22 (the risen Christ breathes on his disciples) or in the Pentecostal promise and fulfilment of Acts 1.8 and 2.4 (see, again, note 3, Chap. 7); and one might expect at any rate the latter to have been intended to represent their endowment with Spirit once for all. Yet, by the time we reach Acts 4.31, they are experiencing a kind of second Pentecost. So, too, believers, who, by definition, have the Spirit already, and in a distinctively Christian manner, are described as subsequently filled with Spirit again for some special crisis or need—Peter, for instance, in Acts 4.8, Stephen in Acts 6.8 (cf. verse 5 and 7.55), or Paul in Acts 13.9. This sort of thing is comparable with the Old Testament story of Joshua's 'ordination' as Moses' successor, when already endowed with spirit. In Num. 27.18–20, the LORD instructs Moses: 'Take Joshua son of Nun, a man endowed with spirit; lay your hand on him and set him before Eleazar the priest and all the community. Give him his commission in their presence, and delegate some of your authority [Hebrew, 'glory' or 'dignity'] to him, so that all the community of the Israelites may obey him.' This, admittedly, does not mention spirit a second time; but the commissioning evidently implies equipment with special ability, and not merely authorisation. So it is that the confirmation of the baptised into full communicant membership and the ordination of a priest for the ministry of the Word and the Sacraments, and the consecration of a Bishop can all be recognised as occasions on which persons already endowed with the Spirit are nevertheless equipped with a special accession of spiritual ability for the tasks to which they are called. God does equip persons already devoted to him, so that they may rise to special opportunities and special demands; and one outstanding aspect of such equipment is empowering for 'mission'—the spiritual incitement and enabling by which one is sent out for evangelism. This is especially evident in the Acts, at such moments, for instance, as the start of the Pauline missions in 13.2, when the Spirit's voice is heard saying '"Set Barnabas and Saul apart for me, to do the work to which I have called them". Then, after further fasting and prayer, they laid their hands on them and let them go.' On their return (Acts 14.26) they are described as having fulfilled the task for which they had been commended to the grace of God.

But how a sacramental occasion is related to the coming of the Spirit it is still not easy to define. Notoriously, as we have seen, the story in Acts 8 distances the baptism of the Samaritans by some days from their subsequent reception of the Spirit on the imposition of apostolic hands. But, conversely, Cornelius and his friends receive the Spirit in advance of baptism (Acts 10.44, 11.15). Other passages, already quoted, seem to hold the water and the Spirit more closely together: John 3.5, Acts 2.38, 1 Cor. 6.11, 12.13 (though there is a measure of doubt in these passages—see pp. 77 f. above). The imposition of hands, perplexingly, is sometimes mentioned, sometimes not. In addition to Acts 8.17 just referred to, the seven men appointed to minister to the Hellenist widows receive the laying on of hands (Acts 6.6) for their specialised ministry. (This is not the ministry of deacons in the later, technical sense, and they are never so styled.) The devout Jewish believer Ananias lays hands on Paul after his encounter with Christ on the Damascus road—but this is apparently for the restoration of his sight (Acts 9.17). The missionaries of Acts 13 are commissioned by the imposition of hands, in the passage just quoted. In Acts 19.6 Paul lays hands on those whom he has just caused to receive Christian baptism. Timothy is spoken of as thus commissioned (1 Tim. 4.14, 2 Tim. 1.6), and is himself instructed not to lay hands hastily on anyone (1 Tim. 5.22, though it is not stated what was the purpose of this imposition of hands. Was it for absolution, or for some sort of commissioning?).

Much of the detail, then, in the New Testament accounts is obscure. What is clear is that the imposition of hands (which already had an important place in the practice of non-Christian Judaism) is often a recognised 'focus' of special endowment with Spirit. The Church's subsequent use of it in confirmation, ordination, and consecration, as well as, at unspecified times, for healing, absolving, commissioning and the like, is in line with this practice.

It would be out of place and out of proportion to pursue here the question what constitutes authoritative commissioning for the Christian ministry of the Word and Sacraments, with its accompanying divisive debates about apostolic succession. It is, however, relevant to the understanding of the Spirit to inquire a little further into a matter already touched on, namely, the relation in time between a sacramental moment and the moment of the perception of the Spirit's presence. No mortal can say precisely when the Spirit of God visits him: this is not to be pinned down in time. But even the moment of one's perceiving the visitation is variable. We

return to the example mentioned in the preceding chapter.
When a man and woman are declared to be husband and wife
because they have pledged their troth to each other and have
given and received a ring, what has happened? A legal moment
has come and gone, certainly. Before it, they were not legally
wed; after it, they are. But in terms of their relation of love to
one another, love (one hopes) began long before this moment;
and certainly, all being well, it will continue to mature ever
after. Certainly, the couple may have *felt* no new or further
access of love at the particular moment of marriage. And it
may well be that, so far as a particular point in time is concerned, the sexual consummation of their mutual relationship
may be, on the emotional level, incomparably more significant. But all this in no way reduces the importance of the
public sacramental moment (which happens also, in an established Church, to be the legal moment). It has its particular
function at a particular moment in a long process of the matur-
ing of a relationship which, as a whole, cannot be pinned down
to dates and times at all. The sacrament is a 'focus' for God's
gracious promises in their relation to persons and in their relation also, very importantly, to the Christian community to
which the persons belong. But there may well be a kind of
'staggering' of the factors in the experience, such that the
emotional or volitional implementing of the relationship does
not coincide with this formal expression of it in a public sacrament or a visible gesture. The sacrament may take place
before, at, or after other factors. But it constitutes a vital part
of the whole process. Even so simple a gesture as a handshake
or a kiss may act as a 'focus' for the beginning, the clinching, or
the climax of a relationship. More often it is a repeated renewal, just as the Eucharist is the repetitive form and the constant renewal of that of which Baptism, which is not
repeatable, symbolises the once-for-all character. Sacraments
need not be simultaneous with that which they 'focus', any
more than a human relationship need be felt with uniform
emotional intensity at every moment. They are the conscious,
considered 'focal points' of a protracted—perhaps a time-
less—reality.

So much, then, for successive special endowments, and for

the question of the relation between a sacrament and the long process of which it forms the 'focal point'. But we have come round full circle to the dilemma already alluded to earlier. Paul can appeal to the Spirit's presence as evidence that his friends belong to God and that God's purposes are going to be consummated for them. He appears to take the Spirit's presence as axiomatic and evident, and deduces the rest from it. It is the same in 1 John 3.24 ('. . . we know it from the Spirit he has given us'), 4.13 ('Here is the proof that we dwell in him and he dwells in us: he has imparted his Spirit to us'). But if one discounts as inessential such phenomena as may be readily tested—visible deeds of power and audible utterance of a 'spiritual' kind—how is one to be sure of the Spirit's presence? Love, joy, peace, and the rest—the 'inward' characteristics of the Spirit's presence—are evident enough over a period, and it is all too easy to be aware of their absence; but they cannot be instantly tested or pinned down. It is hardly surprising, then, that one reaches a situation opposite to the Pauline, where all that can be tested and certified is the ritual of baptism or the laying on of hands, and where a counsellor may be heard virtually to say 'Don't expect to notice any difference: just believe you have received the Spirit!' In this dilemma, must not the people of God welcome all visible and audible signs, but, at the same time, be vigilant to avoid using them as exclusive tests such as to unchurch those who have not received them? And, conversely, must they not trust God for his presence, even when it is not signalised openly, and even in periods of wandering in the desert, but be vigilant to avoid complacent assumptions of aliveness when there is only deadness?

Finally, there is another most urgent consideration, which is to make sure that allegedly spiritual experiences and states are genuinely Christian. G. S. Hendry, speaking of 'enthusiasm' in the technical sense not of zeal, simply, but of being caught up by inspiration, writes:[11]

> 'Enthusiasm exalts the sovereign freedom of the Spirit over against the Roman Catholic tendency to canalize and domesticate the Spirit in the Church [n.b. the date of the book is 1957!], but in such a way as virtually to sever

the connection between the mission of the Spirit and the historical Christ. The emphasis is laid on the immediate, subjective experience of the Spirit in the individual rather than on his appropriation of "the redemption purchased by Christ" in the work of his incarnate life. The real attitude of enthusiasm (and this was openly avowed in its more extravagant forms such as Montanism and Joachimism) is that the dispensation of the Spirit superseded the historical revelation of Christ. This is concealed in modern forms of enthusiasm beneath an appearance of devotion to the Christ of the New Testament, but it is not really changed; for the historical revelation of Christ is treated as the stimulus to a subjective spiritual experience in the individual, not as itself the content of that experience. The spiritualist individual experiences his own conversion and the resultant spiritual glow rather than Jesus Christ and him crucified; when he bears his testimony, it is to speak of his new-found peace and happiness rather than to confess that Jesus Christ is Lord.'

This reflects faithfully what was evidently Paul's concern for the Corinthian Christians, and it is a warning needing constantly to be heeded. If this chapter ends on this negative note, it is in no way to suggest that, ultimately, the so-called charismatic experience is to be looked at with suspicion, still less frowned on. It is only to underline the fact that *corruptio optimi pessima*—nothing is worse than a perverted form of the best. The presence of the Spirit of God, which can be a robust, tough, un-sentimental matter, can nevertheless be quickly and subtly attacked and undermined precisely at its most attractive level. The Psalmist's cry, 'Do not take thy Holy Spirit from me!', which concerned us so near the beginning of this book, is a salutary prayer with which to end.

Epilogue

ANY serious investigation into a great and important subject is bound to land itself in a tangle of words. Words are feeble things—never adequate for the job; yet priceless things—seldom dispensable. They are dangerous things, for they are so fascinating that they tempt the user to linger with them and treat them as ends instead of means. But the Word became flesh; and a word that is not in some way implemented goes sour and becomes a liability instead of an asset. All this talk about Spirit and spirit has been an attempt to focus the lens as sharply as possible upon the functions of that momentous word. If it has thereby helped anybody to understand even a little better certain aspects of the living God's infinitely variegated wisdom and work and to enter into them more actively, it will have served its purpose. But if it has only confused the reader, or tempted him to go on weaving words instead of entering more richly into the experience they serve to define— God forgive us both!

Material for Prayers

WHAT follows is a series of prayers (or thoughts towards God) based on New Testament material relating to the Holy Spirit. No attempt has been made to turn them into such form as might be worthy of public liturgy, or to give them the elegance and grace necessary if they are to be frequently used, even in private. They are in pedestrian prose. They aim simply at faithfully reflecting and staying within New Testament conceptions of Spirit. It is hoped that they could prove to be the raw material of a biblical liturgy of the Spirit. They are broken down where necessary into short phrases, in the interests of showing the source or authority for each phrase.

Mark 14.36
>   Father, dear Father, your Son Jesus Christ addressed you like this,
Matt. 6.9 (6.1–7.11)
>   and taught his disciples to do so too.
Mark 1.11
>   Let the Spirit who confirmed his sonship
Rom. 8.15, Gal. 4.6
>   give us the trust and the courage to say the same words;
Rom. 8:5–11
>   and not to say them only, but to live them, and to accept the revolutionary consequences: Father, dear Father, your will, not ours, be done.
1 Cor. 12.3
>   May the Spirit enable us to confess Jesus as Lord.

Matt. 4.1–11, Luke 4.1–13, and *passim*
> May Christ's Spirit-directed choices be foremost—bringing time, always, for persons and a refusal to be tyrannised by things.

2 Cor. 3.18
> May we become more and more like Christ because of the Spirit's presence.

Rom. 8.26
> We do not know how to pray.

Rom. 8.31–39
> We trust our Lord Jesus Christ, who is your understanding of us—an understanding far deeper than our own understanding of ourselves. Christ, who is your understanding of us, intercedes for us.

Rom. 8.26
> When words fail, the Spirit, too, intercedes for us, interpreting our groaning.

Eph. 6.18, Jude 20
> It is by the Holy Spirit that we are enabled to pray.

2 Cor. 3.12, 17 f.
> Unexpectedly, therefore, and for no merit of our own, we enjoy a great confidence, because of the direct access to God given us by Jesus Christ in the Holy Spirit.

Mark 1.12, Rom. 8.14
> Father, let us be led by the Spirit,

Gal. 5.16
> and by the Spirit's power let our conduct be shaped.

Rom. 8.13
> By the Spirit's power let us kill dead in ourselves all that is not your will.

1 Cor. 6.19 f.
> Let us recall the tremendous fact that each Christian's body is a shrine of the Holy Spirit. We do not belong to ourselves but to you.

Eph. 6.17, Mark 13.11, Acts 6.10, Rev. 1.16, 2.12, 16, 19.15.
> Let us grasp and wield the Spirit's sword, obeying your words and speaking them.

1 Cor. 2.9 ff.
> Father, we throw open our spirits to your Spirit, so that

we may know what, by ourselves, we cannot know; and, having the mind of Christ, may see your mysteries, and be transformed.

1 Cor. 14.29, 1 Thess. 5.21, 2 Thess. 2.2, 1 John 4.1 ff.

Show us the difference between false claims to inspiration, and the Spirit's authentic voice.

Rev. 2.7, etc. (cf. 19.10)

Let us listen to what the Spirit is saying, of judgement and of hope, to each Christian congregation through your spokesmen, wherever and whoever they may be.

Rom. 8.15 f., Gal. 4.6

Father, we rejoice because your Spirit's presence proves that Christ is here

1 Cor. 12.3

as Lord.

Gal. 5.22, 6.8, cf. 1 Cor. 13; 14.1; Rom. 5.5

The Spirit's signs are love, joy, peace, patience, generosity, goodness, trustworthiness, tolerance, self-control,

Acts 2 and *passim*; 1 Cor. 14

and many other precious gifts: among them, tongues and healing.

1 Thess. 5.19

Help us not to quench the Spirit.

Rom. 8.23; 2 Cor. 1.22, 5.5, Eph. 1.14

In this presence of the Holy Spirit, you give us a foretaste and a pledge of what is to come.

2 Cor. 1.21

As a king is anointed for his sacred task,

Acts 2.4, etc.; Acts 13.2, etc. Eph. 1.13, 4.30

you fill us with ability to discharge the tasks to which you call us, as you seal us for your own.

Acts 5.32

It is those who obey you to whom you give the Holy Spirit.

Eph. 4.30

Keep us faithful, and let us not grieve,

Matt. 12.31, Mark 3.29, Luke 12.10, Acts 7.51, 1 Cor. 3.17, 6.19

or sin against,

Acts 5.3

> or lie to your Holy Spirit.

Acts 18.25, Rom. 12.11

> By the Holy Spirit let us glow with enthusiasm and zest.

Eph. 5.18–20

> By the Holy Spirit make us delirious with your praise and adoration.

John 14–16

> Father, may the Holy Spirit, as Champion of your People, call to our minds the words of Jesus, search us, judge us, instruct us,

Acts 11.28, 16.7, 21.11

> guide us into truth,

John 20.21, Acts 1.8, 13.2 (cf. the shortest ending of Mark in certain Greek texts: 'Jesus himself sent out through them from east to west the sacred and imperishable proclamation of eternal salvation'.)

> and send us out beyond our own circle to be spokesmen for Christ.

John 3.5, 7.39

> Father, let us in deed and word know the new birth,

Acts 2.38, 8.17, 9.17–19, etc.

> the baptism with the Spirit,

Rom. 8.11

> which is given us in Jesus Christ, crucified and raised.

1 Cor. 3.16

> Together we are the Temple in which God is worshipped and in which the Spirit dwells;

1 Cor. 6.19

> each of us is a shrine for the Holy Spirit:

Eph. 2.22

> so may we be built, together with our fellow-Christians, into a holy Temple by the Spirit,

Eph. 4.3

> eagerly preserving the unity which the Spirit brings.

Eph. 5.25–27

> In Christ's Bride, the Church,

Rev. 22.17

> the Spirit's voice says, 'Come, Lord Jesus! Come!'

2 Cor. 13.13

May the graciousness shown and put into action by the Lord Jesus Christ, and the love put forth by God, and a joint sharing in the Holy Spirit, all belong to us.

Editions and Notations

QUOTATIONS from the Bible are largely, though not invariably, in the version called the New English Bible.

The *'Apostolic Fathers'* (see pp. 60, 65) can be conveniently read in the Loeb edition, or in M. Staniforth's translation (see note 25, Chap. 3).

The *Dead Sea Scrolls* from the caves of Wadi Qumran are most easily consulted in the English translation and edition by G. Vermes (Penguin Books 1962 and subsequent editions). In the notes here, they are cited by abbreviations in common use, 1Q standing for a document from cave number one at Qumran. Following 1Q, H stands for *Hodayoth*, the Hymns or Psalms of Praise, M for *Milchamah*, the 'War Scroll', S for *Serek*, the so-called Manual of Discipline. A bracketed reference to the page in Vermes' translation is added.

Eusebius of Caesarea, the Church historian (circa AD 260 to 340), is available in the Loeb edition.

Philo, the Alexandrine Jewish writer (in Greek) (circa 20 BC to circa AD 50), is cited by the Latin titles commonly in use for his treatises. He may be conveniently consulted in the Loeb edition.

The so-called *Psalms of Solomon* (in the Greek version of the Jewish Scriptures, though not in the English Apocrypha) may be read in translation in R. H. Charles, ed., *The Apocrypha and Pseudepigrapha of the Old Testament* (Oxford: University Press 1913; reprinted 1963).

Abbreviations

AV	Authorised Version (the 'King James Bible')
CBQ	*The Catholic Biblical Quarterly*
ET	*The Expository Times* (Edinburgh)
JBL	*The Journal of Biblical Literature* (Missoula: University of Montana)
ibid.	*ibidem*, 'in the same place'
id.	*idem*, 'the same'
init.	(*ad*) *initium*, '(at) the beginning'
in loc.	*in loco*, 'at the place (in question)'
JTS	*The Journal of Theological Studies* (Oxford)
NEB	The New English Bible
Nov Test	*Novum Testamentum* (Leiden)
NTS	*New Testament Studies* (Cambridge)
sv, svv	*sub verbo, verbis*, 'under the word or words (in question', as a dictionary entry)
RSV	The Revised Standard Version
RV	The Revised Version

Notes

CHAPTER I

[1] See the excellent discussion in F. W. Dillistone, *The Holy Spirit in the Life of Today* (London/Edinburgh: Canterbury Press 1946), pp. 11–17.

[2] For the association of Spirit with purification, see IQS III.7 f., IV. 21 f. (Vermes 75, 77 f.), IQH XVI. 12 (Vermes 197).

[3] There is a huge literature on this; but see, e.g., T. F. Glasson, 'Water, Wind and Fire (Luke III.16)', *NTS* 3 (1956/7), 69 ff.

[4] See P. D. Miller, 'Fire in the Mythology of Canaan and Israel', *CBQ* 27 (1965), for the background of Amos 7.4, etc.

CHAPTER II

[1] *The Christian Experience of the Holy Spirit* (London: Nisbet 1928), 123.

[2] See Rom. 7.23, 25, 12.2, Eph. 4.23; and, negatively, Rom. 1.28, Eph. 4.17.

[3] *The Holy Spirit in Christian Theology* (London: SCM 1957), 34.

[4] Perhaps the same sort of thing is happening (also in Rom. 8), when Paul speaks first of *our* having the 'outlook' (*phronēma*) either of the flesh or of the Spirit (verse 6), and then (verses 26 f.) seems to identify the outlook of the Spirit with the Holy Spirit's intercessions *on our behalf.*

[5] See IQS III. 18 ff. (Vermes 75 f.).

[6] J. Richards, *But Deliver Us From Evil* (London: Darton, Longman and Todd 1974), contains a bibliography. But the distinction between praying God for the release of a victim and commanding an evil being to depart is sometimes overlooked. Those who condemn or criticise the latter are sometimes misunderstood as disparaging the former.

[7] Cf. IQH I. 8 f. (Vermes 150), IV. 31 (Vermes 163).

[8] See M. E. Isaacs, *The Concept of Spirit: a Study of Pneuma in Hellenistic Judaism and its Bearing on the New Testament* (London: Heythrop Monographs I, 1976), 45 (init.), 56. Philo, *de opificio mundi* 131, illustrates the idea of Spirit as a cohesive force.

[9] E. A. Speiser, *Genesis* (Anchor Bible Commentary, New York: Doubleday 1964) *in loc.*, objects to translating by merely 'mighty'; rather, he says it should be 'divine'; but he accepts that it probably means 'wind' rather than 'spirit'.

¹⁰ Cf. *The Odes and Psalms of Solomon.* (ed. J. Rendel Harris, Cambridge: University Press 1911), 28.1 f., on p. 128: 'As the wings of doves over their nestlings'. See also (a random example) Gen. 1.2 in the Targum of Pseudo-Jonathan, in J. Bowker, *The Targums and Rabbinic Literature* (Cambridge: University Press 1973), 95: '. . . *the* spirit of mercies from before God blew *upon the face of the waters.*'

¹¹ C. E. Raven never tired of urging this cosmic scope of Christian concern. See his Gifford lectures, *Science and Religion*, 2 vols. (Cambridge: University Press 1953).

¹² J. Rendel Harris, *The Origin of the Prologue to St John's Gospel* (Cambridge: University Press 1917), 38, quoted by M. E. Isaacs (as in note 8, Chap. 2), 136. This is where C. E. Raven (as in note 11) tended, perhaps, to misconstrue biblical *usage*, even if we may wholeheartedly agree with his interpretation of the *implications* of biblical theology. See, however, M. Green, *I Believe in the Holy Spirit* (London: Hodder and Stoughton 1975), 28, challenging the minimising position which I am adopting with regard to specifically biblical usage; and A. M. Ramsey, *Holy Spirit* (London: SPCK 1977), 123.

CHAPTER III

¹ For Jewish apocalyptic literature in particular, see H. B. Swete, *The Holy Spirit in the New Testament* (London: Macmillan, 1909), Note Q, 398 ff. For instances in the Targums, see J. Bowker (as in note 10, Chap. 2), 93 ff.

² In addition to the 'standard' use in connection with revelation (as e.g., in IQH XII. 11 f. (Vermes 189)), see IQS III. 6 f. (Vermes 75), IV. 21 (Vermes 77 f.), IQH VII. 6 f. (Vermes 173), IX. 32 (Vermes 182), XVI. 7, 9, 12 (Vermes 196 f.).

³ See R. Birch Hoyle, article 'Spirit (Holy), Spirit of God', in J. Hastings' *Encyclopaedia of Religion and Ethics* (Edinburgh: T. and T. Clark 1908–), 789.

⁴ 1QMX. 10 (Vermes 136). But this is controverted. See a discussion in C. F. D. Moule, *The Origin of Christology* (Cambridge: University Press 1977), 13 f.

⁵ On the other hand, it must be admitted that the so-called Psalms of Solomon, belonging to a religious group shortly before the Christian era, which are extant in Greek but appear to have been originally written in Hebrew, use the terms *hosios* ('pious', probably = Hebrew *ḥasid*) and *dikaios* ('righteous'); but they do not use *hagios* in the way in question, unless it be at 17.43, where, however, the reference is not necessarily to the members of this group. At 17.26, 32, the word is used merely in its ordinary, adjectival way.

⁶ On this section, see G. Kretschmar, *Studien zur Frühchristlichen Trinitätstheologie (Beiträge zur historischen Theologie*, Hrsg. G. Ebeling, 21. Tübingen: Mohr 1956); and C. F. D. Moule, *The New Testament and the Trinity, ET* lxxviii.1 (Oct. 1976), 16 ff.

⁷ See C. H. Dodd, *A Hidden Parable in the Fourth Gospel*, in *More New*

Testament Studies (Manchester: University Press 1968), 30 ff.; J. Jeremias, *New Testament Theology*; (Eng. trans., London: SCM 1971), 59 ff.; J. A. T. Robinson, *The Human Face of God* (London: SCM 1973), 186 ff.

⁸ *Not* I John 5.7 f., where the trinitarian formula in the AV is clearly a late interpolation. See commentaries *in loc.*

⁹ See G. Kittel† and G. Friedrich, edd., *Theological Dictionary of the New Testament* (Eng. trans. by G. W. Bromiley, Grand Rapids: Eerdmans 1964–), v. 955.

¹⁰ On this section, see B. Lindars and S. S. Smalley, edd., *Christ and Spirit in the New Testament* (Cambridge: University Press 1973), and J. D. G. Dunn, *Jesus and the Spirit* (London: SCM 1975).

¹¹ See J. D. G. Dunn, '2 Corinthians 3.17—"the Lord is the Spirit"', *JTS* n.s. xxi (1970), 309 ff.; C. F. D. Moule, '2 Cor. 3.18ᵇ, *kathaper apo kuriou pneumatos*', in H. Baltensweiler und B. Reicke, Hrsgg., *Neues Testament und Geschichte* (*Oscar Cullmann zum 70. Geburtstag*) (Zürich: Theologischer Verlag/Tübingen: J. C. B. Mohr 1972), 231 ff.

¹² See the discussion in H. Berkhof, *The Doctrine of the Holy Spirit* (London: Epworth Press 1964), 25 with 28. I do not think that all the identifications on p. 25 are correctly mad; but p. 28 contains a wise and balanced statement.

¹³ See, e.g., J. B. Lightfoot, *St Paul's Epistle to the Galatians* (London: Macmillan 1884), *in loc.*

¹⁴ 'Christianity is the most revolutionary creed in the world because it seeks a revolution in man', A. M. Ramsey in *The Times*, 21 Nov. 1968, quoted by Garth Lean, *Rebirth of a Nation?* (Poole: Blandford Press 1976), 64. Cf. A. M. Ramsey again as in note 12, Chap. 2, 131.

¹⁵ For a summary of much previous research, and a slight modification in this particular respect, see J. Jeremias, *New Testament Theology*, i (Eng. trans., London: SCM 1971), 61 ff. (66).

¹⁶ *The Authorised Daily Prayer Book*, Eng. trans., S. Singer†, new ed. I. Brodie (London: Eyre and Spottiswoode 1962), e.g., p. 57 (Morning Service). But the plain 'Our Father' (*abinu*) is also found, e.g., p. 48 (Morning Service).

¹⁷ See E. Käsemann, *An die Römer* (Tübingen: J. C. B. Mohr 1973), *in loc.*

¹⁸ M. E. Isaacs (as in note 8, Chap. 2), 102 (I have substituted 'authority' for her Greek *exousia*); cf. 118.

¹⁹ See G. Stählin, '*To pneuma Iesou* (Apostelgeschichte 16.7)', in B. Lindars and S. S. Smalley, edd., *Christ and Spirit* (as in note 10, Chap. 3), 229 ff.

²⁰ Cf. M. E. Isaacs (as in note 8, Chap. 2), 84, 86 *init.*

²¹ See discussions in M. Black, *Romans* (London: Oliphants 1973), 127; E. Käsemann (as in vote 17, Chap. 3), 222 f.; C. E. B. Cranfield, *The Epistle to the Romans*, vol. i (Edinburgh: T. and T. Clark 1975), 411 f.

²² There is a huge literature on this. See R. E. Brown, 'The Paraclete in the Fourth Gospel', *NTS* 13.2 (Jan. 1967), 113 ff., and *id.*, *The Gospel according to John*, xiii–xxi (Anchor Bible Commentary, New York: Doubleday 1970), 1135 ff.

[23] H. Berkhof (as in note 12, Chap. 3), 38.

[24] G. S. Hendry (as in note 3, Chap. 2), 32. Cf. W. D. Davies, *The Gospel and the Land: Early Christianity and Jewish Territorial Doctrine* (Berkeley: University of California Press 1974), 301 f.

[25] Ephesians 9.1, trans. M. Staniforth, *Early Christian Writings: The Apostolic Fathers* (Penguin Books 1968), 78.

[26] M. E. Isaacs (as in note 8, Chap. 2), 114.

[27] For this section, see especially those parts by E. Schweizer of the articles *pneuma* and *sarx* in the *Theological Dictionary* (as in note 9, Chap. 3), vi, 389 ff., vii, 98 ff., 119 ff.

[28] For this and other illuminating points, see S. C. Neill, *The Wrath and the Peace of God* (Christian Literature Society for India (United Society for Christian Literature), Madras/Bangalore/Colombo 1944), 65 ff.

CHAPTER IV

[1] See F. L. Cross†, ed., *The Oxford Dictionary of the Christian Church* (2nd ed., revised by E. A. Livingstone, Oxford: University Press 1974), *s.v.*; H. B. Swete, *The Holy Spirit in the Ancient Church* (London: Macmillan 1912), 287 ff.

[2] As in note 12, Chap. 3, 10 f.

[3] See C. Stead, *Divine Substance* (Oxford: University Press 1977), 223 ff.

[4] See C. Stead (as in note 3, Chap. 4), 190 ff.

[5] For the meaning of such terms, again see C. Stead (as in note 3, Chap. 4).

[6] Edward Gibbon, *The History of the Decline and Fall of the Roman Empire.* In the edition published in 1905 by Methuen, London, see vol. ii, p. 352.

[7] See H. Berkhof (as in note 12, Chap. 3), 110.

[8] See H. B. Swete (as in note 1, Chap. 4), 174, note 2, 223, 287 f., etc.

[9] As in note 1, Chap. 4, 371.

[10] See H. B. Swete, *On the History of the Doctrine of the Procession of the Holy Spirit from the Apostolic Age to the Death of Charlemagne* (Cambridge: Deighton, Bell and Co./London: George Bell and Sons 1876), 2.

[11] As in note 1, Chap. 4, 371.

[12] I am grateful to Mr R. V. Kerr of Pembroke College, Cambridge, for providing me with facts and comments about this, and for referring me to J. Gill's *The Council of Florence* (Cambridge: University Press 1959).

[13] Text in A. Hahn and G. L. Hahn, *Bibliothek der Glaubensregeln der Alten Kirche* (Breslau: Morgenstern 1897), 176.

[14] 'The Essence of Christianity—IV. A Personal View', *ET* lxxxvii.5 (Feb. 1976), 132 ff. (135).

[15] Augustine, *de trinitate* VI. 5.7 (Migne's *Patrologia Latina* vol. 42 Col. 928), *commune aliquid est Patris et Filii;* XV. 27, 50. (*ib.* col. 1097) *communio quaedam consubstantialis* (cited by K. Barth, *Die kirchliche Dogmatik* 1.1 (München: Chr. Kaiser 1932), 492 f.), Eng. trans. (Edinburgh: T. and T. Clark 1936) 537.

[16] *Atonement and Personality* (London: Murray 1901), 173 f., cited by A. M. Ramsey, as in note 12, Chap. 2, 120.

[17] *The Doctrine of the Trinity* (New York/Nashville: Abingdon Press 1958), 139.

[18] As in note 17, Chap. 4, 106; and, for his critique of D. Sayers, 135 ff.

[19] J. V. Taylor, *The Go-Between God* (London: SCM 1972), 83. This criticism is not for a moment to suggest that Bishop Taylor's book is not a profound and suggestive one.

CHAPTER V

[1] See *The Oxford Dictionary of the Christian Church* (as in note 1, Chap. 4) *s.vv.*

[2] See H. B. Swete (as in note 1, Chap. 4), 291 ff., 398.

[3] On the docetism of the Fourth Gospel, see E. Käsemann, *The Testament of Jesus* (Eng. trans., London: SCM 1968); but this has not gone unanswered, e.g., by G. Bornkamm, 'Zur Interpretation des Johannes-Evangeliums: eine Auseinandersetzung mit Ernst Käsemanns Schrift "Jesu letzter Wille nach Johannes 17"', in *Geschichte und Glaube* I (Gesammelte Aufsätze Band III) (München: Chr. Kaiser 1968), 104 ff., and by J. D. G. Dunn, *Unity and Diversity in the New Testament* (London: SCM 1977), 300 ff.

[4] See G. B. Caird, *Paul's Letters from Prison* (New Clarendon Bible, Oxford: University Press 1976), 191.

[5] See E. Schweizer, *Der Brief an die Kolosser* (Zürich: Benziger Verlag/ Neukirchen-Vluyn: Neukirchener Verlag 1976), 108.

[6] Ed. J. Hick (London: SCM 1977).

[7] 'The Significance of the Historical Existence of Jesus for Faith', in R. Morgan and M. Pye, edd., Ernst Troeltsch: *Writings on theology and religion* (London: Duckworth 1977), 182 ff.

[8] Ed. M. Green (London: Hodder and Stoughton 1977).

[9] As in note 3, Chap. 4.

[10] See, however, K. Ward, 'Incarnation or Inspiration—a False Dichotomy?', *Theology* lxxx.676 (July 1977), 251 ff. (with correspondence, *Theology* lxxx.678 (Nov. 1977), 444 f., and lxxxi.679 (Jan. 1978), 47 f.). Professor G. W. H. Lampe's Bampton Lectures, *God as Spirit* (Oxford: University Press 1977), came into my hands too late to be adequately used in this discussion. But he, too, challenges this dichotomy with great forcefulness.

[11] Much important light is thrown on the matter by M. Hengel, *The Son of God* (Eng. trans., London: SCM 1976). See also C. F. D. Moule, *The Origin of Christology* (Cambridge: University Press 1977).

[12] See C. F. D. Moule, 'The manhood of Jesus in the New Testament', in S. W. Sykes and J. P. Clayton, edd., *Christ, Faith and History: Cambridge Studies in Christology* (Cambridge: University Press 1972), 95 ff.

[13] As in note 12, Chap. 3, 20.

[14] See M. E. Isaacs (as in note 8, Chap. 2), 51.

[15] See M. E. Isaacs (as in note 8, Chap. 2), 49.

[16] Cited by M. E. Isaacs (as in note 8, Chap. 2), 116.

[17] See, e.g., the selections in J. Bowker (as in note 10, Chap. 2).

[18] G. R. Beasley-Murray, *The Book of Revelation* (New Century Bible, Exeter: Oliphants 1974), 276; G. B. Caird, *The Revelation of St John the Divine* (London: A. and C. Black 1966), 237 f.

[19] G. B. Caird (as in note 18, Chap. 5), 238.

[20] Discussed by G. Stählin (as in note 19, Chap. 3).

[21] So Philo, e.g. *quis rerum divinarum heres* 259 (Loeb ed. iv, p. 416/417), *de specialibus legibus* IV.49 (Loeb ed. viii, pp. 36/37, 38/39); and an early Christian example (about AD 177) is Athenagoras, *legatio* 9 (translation by J. H. Crehan in *Ancient Christian Writers*, edd. Quasten and Plumpe (Westminster, Maryland: Newman Press/London: Longmans, Green and Co. 1956), 39.

[22] Loeb ed., trans. K. Lake, i.324 ff.

[23] See C. A. Pierce, *Conscience in the New Testament* (London: SCM 1955), 108 (for summary); and article *sunoida, suneidēsis* by Maurer in *Theological Dictionary* (as in note 9, Chap. 3), vii, 899 ff.

[24] So B. B. Warfield, articles published in the 19th and 20th centuries, collected as *The Inspiration and Authority of the Bible*, ed. S. G. Craig (Philadelphia: the Presbyterian and Reformed Publishing Co. 1948), 133.

[25] See, e.g. F. F. Bruce, 'The History of New Testament Study', in I. H. Marshall, ed., *New Testament Interpretation* (Exeter: Paternoster 1977), 21 ff.

[26] See valuable discussions by D. H. Kelsey, *The Uses of Scripture in Recent Theology* (London: SCM 1975/Philadelphia: Fortress 1975), and by J. Barr, *Fundamentalism* (London: SCM 1977).

[27] See note 21, Chap. 5 above. Philo says the same without this particular analogy.

CHAPTER VI

[1] *Sermo* 267, 4, quoted by H. Berkhof (as in note 12, Chap. 3), 42.

[2] *Kirchliche Dogmatik* (as in note 15, Chap. 4), IV. 2 (1955), 695; cf. IV. 1 (1953), 718. (Eng. trans., *Church Dogmatics*, IV. 2 (Edinburgh: T. and T. Clark 1958), 614; cf. *id*. IV. 1 (1956), 643.).

[3] See the discussion in *The Origin of Christology* (as in note 4, Chap. 3), 69 ff., with bibliography there.

[4] C. F. D. Moule, 'The Judgement Theme in The Sacraments', in W. D. Davies and D. Daube, edd., *The Background of the New Testament and its Eschatology* (Cambridge: University Press 1956), 464 ff.

[5] Eusebius, *Historia Ecclesiastica* 10.5. 10–12 (Loeb ed. ii, p. 450/451) does use this phrase.

[6] See the discussion in *The Origin of Christology* (as in note 4, Chap. 3), 54 ff., with bibliography there.

[7] *Kirchliche Dogmatik* (as in note 15, Chap. 4), I.1 (1932), 476, Eng. trans.,

The Doctrine of the Word of God (*Prolegomena to Church Dogmatics,* being Vol. I, part I) (Edinburgh: T. and T. Clark 1936), 519: 'The formula *en pneumati,* so frequent in Paul, signifies the thought, action, and language of man, as taking place by participation in God's revelation. It is pretty much the subjective correlate to *en Christō(i),* which objectively signifies the same material content.'

[8] E.g., by L. Newbigin *The Household of God* (London: SCM 1953), 95 (quoted by J. V. Taylor (as in note 19, Chap. 4), 199); and by S. Tugwell, *Did you receive the Spirit?* (London: Darton, Longman and Todd 1972).

[9] As in note 3, Chap. 2, 41. Cf. H. W. Robinson (as in note 1, Chap. 2), 146 f., 238 ('. . . the Holy Spirit safeguards . . . the real presence of God in human personality through faith in Christ').

[10] See J. Y. Campbell, '*KOINONIA* and its Cognates in the New Testament', *JBL* li–iv (1932), 352 ff. (reprinted in *Three New Testament Studies* (Leiden: Brill 1965), 1 ff.); and H. Seesemann, *Der Begriff* koinonia *im NT,* Beihefte zur *ZNTW* 14 (Giessen: Töpelmann 1933); and the article *koinos* etc. by Hauck in *Theological Dictionary* (as in note 9, Chap. 3), iii, 789 ff.

[11] R. R. Williams, 'Logic *versus* Experience in the Order of Credal Formulae', *NTS* 1.1 (Sept. 1954), 42 ff.

[12] Cf. G. B. Caird, *Paul's Letters from Prison* (as in note 4, Chap. 5), 73 ff.

[13] Cf. M. E. Isaacs (as in note 8, Chap. 2), 91.

[14] See G. W. H. Lampe, *The Seal of the Spirit* (London: Longmans, Green and Co. 1951); J. D. G. Dunn, *Baptism in the Holy Spirit,* (London: SCM 1970); *id.* 'Spirit and Fire Baptism', *Nov. Test.* 14.2 (April 1972), 81 ff.; J. K. Parratt, 'The Holy Spirit and Baptism', *ET* lxxxii (1971), 26 ff.

[15] *The Gospel of John* (Eng. trans., Oxford: University Press 1971. The original appeared in 1941).

[16] *Baptism in the Holy Spirit* (as in note 14, Chap. 6), 192.

[17] *The Fourth Gospel Interpreted in its Relation to Contemporaneous Religious Currents in Palestine and the Hellenistic-Oriental World* (Uppsala/Stockholm: Almquist and Wicksell 1929), 49.

[18] Surah IV. 157; see the discussion in K. Cragg, *The Call of the Minaret* (New York: Oxford University Press 1956), 294 ff.

[19] See the discussion in J. L. Houlden, *A Commentary on the Johannine Epistles* (London: A. and C. Black 1973), 130 ff.

[20] *The Johannine Epistles* (Moffatt Commentary, London: Hodder and Stoughton 1946), *in loc.*

[21] As in note 12, Chap. 3, 10.

[22] As in note 17, Chap. 4, 145.

[23] Just so, A. Ritschl criticised the hymns for Pentecost in the Lutheran hymn-book of the Hanoverian Church, saying that little mention is made of the Spirit as the creator of a common consciousness and corporate fellowship within the Church. (This is a summary given by R. Birch Hoyle (as in note 3, Chap. 3), 801, of the purport of p. 328 of Ritschl's *A Critical History of the Christian Doctrine of Justification and Reconciliation* (Eng. trans., Edinburgh: Edmonston and Douglas 1872).)

CHAPTER VII

[1] See especially W. J. Hollenweger, *The Pentecostals* (London: SCM 1972). I have not consulted his huge *Handbuch der Pfingstbewegung* (9 vols., 1965, photocopied), which is used by A. D. Galloway, 'Recent Thinking on Christian Beliefs. III. The Holy Spirit', *ET* lxxxviii. 4 (Jan. 1977), 100 ff.

[2] Especially J. D. G. Dunn (as in note 14, Chap. 6) and F. D. Bruner, *A Theology of the Holy Spirit* (Grand Rapids: Eerdmans 1970).

[3] M. M. B. Turner has made a special study of the range of different meanings attached in the New Testament to receiving the Spirit, and he devotes an article to the relation of John 20.22 to the coming of the Spirit as Paraclete: 'The Concept of Receiving the Spirit in John's Gospel', *Vox Evangelica* x (London Bible College 1977), 24 ff. His earlier article, 'The Significance of Spirit Endowment for Paul', *Vox Evangelica* ix (1975), 56 ff., carries out a similar investigation for the Pauline writings. For a different interpretation of John 20.22, see J. D. G. Dunn, *Baptism in the Holy Spirit* (as in note 14, Chap. 6), 173 ff.

[4] See P. Hocken, 'The Significance and Potential of Pentecostalism', in S. Tugwell, P. Hocken, G. Every, J. O. Mills, *New Heaven? New Earth?* (London: Darton, Longman and Todd 1976), 22; and K. S. Hemphill, 'The Pauline concept of charisma: a situational and developmental approach', unpublished Ph.D. dissertation, Cambridge University 1977.

[5] As in note 1, Chap. 7, 102.

[6] The firm of Bagster was founded in 1794, and published polyglot Bibles and reference works. I have never found anyone to tell me the origin of their elegant motto.

[7] In *Disciple* (Lakeland 1976), quoted by S. Barrington-Ward in the Church Missionary Society Newsletter no. 406 (Dec. 1976).

[8] A. Bloom, *School for Prayer* (London: Darton, Longman and Todd 1970), 75, and J. V. Taylor (as in note 19, Chap. 4), 233.

[9] I recount it from memory—and perhaps inaccurately in detail—from conversation with the late J. P. S. R. Gibson, one time Principal of Ridley Hall, Cambridge, and earlier a missionary in Peradeniya, Ceylon.

[10] See J. D. G. Dunn (as in note 10, Chap. 3), 84 ff.

[11] As in note 3, Chap. 2, 68 f.

Index of Authors

Index of References

CPSIA information can be obtained
at www.ICGtesting.com
Printed in the USA
BVHW031533211122
652434BV00007B/186

9 781579 100353